FLY-FISHING
FOR THE
CLUELESS

FLY-FISHING FOR THE CLUELESS

Donald A. Henderson, P.E.

CITADEL PRESS
Kensington Publishing Corp.
http://www.kensingtonbooks.com

CITADEL PRESS BOOKS are published by

Kensington Publishing Corp.
850 Third Avenue
New York, NY 10022

All Kensington titles, imprints, and distributed lines are available at special quantity discounts for bulk purchases for sales promotions, premiums, fund-raising, educational, or institutional use. Special book excerpts or customized printings can also be created to fit specific needs. For details, write or phone the office of the Kensington special sales manager: Kensington Publishing Corp., 850 Third Avenue, New York, NY 10022, attn: Special Sales Department, Phone: 1-800-221-2647

Citadel Press and the Citadel logo are trademarks of Kensington Publishing Corp.

First Citadel Printing: June 2001

10   9   8   7   6   5   4   3   2   1

Printed in the United States of America

Library of Congress Control Number 2001092637

ISBN 0-8065-2196-1

CONTENTS

Preface   vii

Chapter 1   What Fish Feed On—Insects, Minnows,
                and Other Things   1

Chapter 2   Fly Imitations for Fly-Fishing   14

Chapter 3   Fly-Fishing Tackle   26

Chapter 4   Knots and Tackle Assembly   45

Chapter 5   Fly-Fishing Accessories   57

Chapter 6   Fly-Casting   63

Chapter 7   Fly-Fishing Strategies, Reconnaissance,
                and Tactics   75

Chapter 8   The Kind of Fish the Fly-Fisher Fishes For   86

Chapter 9   The First Fly-Fishing Exercise   106

Chapter 10 Saltwater Fly-Fishing   118

Chapter 11 After You Catch the Fish   129

Chapter 12 The Clueless Chef Cooks the Fish   139

Chapter 13 Laws, Ethics, Good Manners, and
                Safety for Good Fishing   150

Fly-Fishing Glossary   161

DEDICATION

To my children, their children, and all curious people, with the hope and prayer that they will find the "be all and end all" of their busy lives with the peace, serenity, humility, and satisfaction that comes with fly-fishing. Satisfaction and happiness are not always easy to measure, but a very old Chinese proverb may sum it up quite well.

If you wish to be happy for an hour, get intoxicated.
If you wish to be happy for three days, get married.
If you wish to be happy for eight days, kill your pig and eat it.
If you wish to be happy forever, learn to fish.

THE FISH

Freshwater Fish	Saltwater Fish
Trout	Bonefish
Bass	Snook
Bluegill	Snapper
Panfish	Grunts
Bream	Mackerel
Suckers	Tarpon

PREFACE

This book is written for those individuals who are curious and interested in learning how to fish with a fly rod and artificial flies, including those who haven't a clue as to how to even start fishing as well as those who have fished for many years with live bait, artificial lures, and heavy saltwater tackle. Fly-fishing is different from any of the more popular methods of fishing and, for those who do fish with a fly rod and artificial flies, much more fun than traditional fishing methods. Compared to other forms of fishing, fly-fishing (with a delicate presentation of a dry fly or a nymph) is much more graceful and even beautiful when practiced in the setting of pristine lakes, streams, and/or saltwater tidal flats of America.

Fly-fishing is the technique or act of angling (fishing) by casting an artificial fly as a lure for the fish. Casting is the technique or act of throwing out a line onto the water with the aid of a rod. An artificial fly is a hook dressed up with fur and feathers to imitate an aquatic insect, a terrestrial insect, or a minnow. When we talk about fly-fishing, we are not talking about the well-known common housefly, *Musca domestica,* or the other common flies, such as the horsefly or the deerfly. The flies we are concerned with are primarily aquatic insects whose life cycles are almost entirely underwater except for the relatively brief periods of their hatches, when they mate above the water so they can lay their eggs in the water for the next generation of flies. The life cycle of the mayfly is typical. The larva that hatches from the egg is called a nymph and lives underwater for as long as two years. When the nymph (larva), which is an immature insect, transforms into a pupa (subimago), it rises to the surface. It is then called an emerging dun until its wings dry out. When the wings dry out and it rises in the air, it is called a spinner (imago). It is called a spinner because as it beats its wings in its nuptial flight, it appears like a spinning propeller when the sunlight or moonlight shines on its wings. This whole process of rising from the surface of the water after the long incubation period and then flying in the air to mate is called the *hatch.* Terrestrial insects that anglers are concerned with are grasshoppers, crickets, ants, etc. Their life cycles are above the water, and they are commonly blown by the wind onto the water. Minnows are immature, or baitfish, which make up a good part of the diet of the larger mature fish. Eggs from female salmon deposited in the stream are a favorite food for steelhead, which is a migrating rainbow trout.

There are five types of artificial flies most often used for fly-fishing, and this book outlines the basic techniques of fishing with them. They are streamers, wet flies, nymphs, dry flies, and eggs, each representing some of the most basic food that fish thrive on. Streamers are imitation minnows, or baitfish. Wet flies are imitation aquatic flies that have just developed wings from the pupa stage but are still underwater. Nymphs are artificial immature flies still in the larva stage, having emerged from the egg. Dry flies are the artificial mature flies with dry wings that float on top of the water, ready to fly. Egg flies are imitation salmon eggs used to fish for salmon and steelhead (rainbow trout). It is of no small importance that fly-fishing is the best way that these important fish foods can be presented to the fish by the angler. The more conventional fishing methods rarely use either artificial or real flies for bait.

The skills needed for fly-fishing are very elementary and can be easily learned by men, women, and even children. Equipment for beginners is most economical. Inexpensive sets of fly rod, reel, line, and leaders (nearly invisible nylon line attached to the end of the fly line) are available from any sporting-goods store for one to get started. The tippet is the relatively thin last 3 or 4 feet of the leader to which the fly is attached. Knowledge, skill, and delicate presentation of the artificial flies are much more important than expensive tackle. Expert fly-casters can even cast well with a broomstick.

If you enjoy the outdoors, like to have fun, desire a genuine communion with nature, and want to engage in one of the most challenging sports ever conceived of in the history of civilization, try the magic of fly-fishing. As President Herbert Hoover once pointed out, "Fishing is the chance to wash one's soul with pure air. It brings meekness and inspiration, reduces our egotism, soothes our troubles and shames our wickedness. It is discipline in the equality of men (and women), for all men (and women) are equal before fish."

Paradoxically, it would be hard to find any other form of recreation that is more shrouded in secrecy and seclusion than the fine

art of fly-fishing. Obfuscation, confusion, mystery, and total apho-
nia with regard to what, how, and especially where a fish might be
caught with a fly rod have been the hallmark of the members of this
all too restrictive (mostly male) community in America and Europe. Such imperious surroundings that have been identified with
fly-fishing have all too often intimidated people who had a sincere
interest in beginning this magnificent sport. Don't be intimidated!
Remember, studies show that for this superb form of recreation,
scenery, solitude, well-being, and contentment, full stringers of fish
are not the number-one priority for angler satisfaction. Hooking,
landing a fish, and taking a good picture are all a bonus. Releasing
that fish adds a lot to the triumph. If you love nature, are up to a
challenge, and want to have fun while you're at it, start fly-fishing.

There is no valid reason why this most therapeutic and relaxing form of recreation cannot be open and available to all who love
the outdoors. The investment is minimal. The rewards for the time
well spent cannot be measured in dollars but will be remembered
for years to come. Contrary to much of the mythology associated
with fly-fishing, it is not difficult to become competent, proficient,
and skillful with the fly rod. Once you learn some of the most fundamental principles of the life cycles of aquatic insects (fish food),
the morphology (life structure) of freshwater and saltwater fish,
and the presentation of artificial flies with a fly rod (casting the fly
to the fish), the fun really begins. This book presents an explanation of these fundamentals.

Women are very important to fly-fishing. For all practical pur-
poses, that's how the sport got started. There is some evidence of fly-
fishing in ancient Greece as early as 300 B.C., and the red hackle, an
artificial fly first described by the Romans, is still used today. Histo-
rians suggest that the beginnings of fly-fishing started in Macedonia
about the third or fourth century B.C., nearly twenty-four hundred
years ago. The historian Aelian (230–170 B.C.) wrote that the Macedonians observed an insect hovering over the water that was not a
wasp, housefly, or bee but something of each of these. He then went
on to say that the Macedonians' feathered imitation of this insect
was made up of two feathers from a cock's wattle fastened to a hook
wrapped in red or crimson wool. Aelian also explained the use of a
very long rod to which a line and a fly were attached to deceive a
"speckled fish" that lived in those waters.

As a practical matter, fly-fishing for sport began in the year 1486, when Dame Juliana Berners, a Benedictine nun who is said to have been the prioress of the Sopwell Nunnery in England, published "The Treatyse of Fysshynge wyth an Angle" in the *Book of St. Albans.* Dame Berners covered such things as the materials for rods, like the middle of green hazel; the top of blackthorn, crabtree, medlar, or juniper; the butt of willow, hazel, or aspen; and the lines of horsehair. She also described the best time of day to fish and, in particular, twelve flies that should be used. She even described a simple code of conduct for fishing on private land and with other anglers. Later, the patron saint of all anglers, Izaak Walton, published his book *The Complete Angler* in 1653. This book was extremely popular, although there wasn't much about fly-fishing in it until 1676, when he asked Charles Cotton, his fishing companion, to write a special section on fly-fishing for the sixth edition. Cotton described in detail how to taper and weave together the various types of horsehair to form a line for rods that was 18 feet long. He also gave a full description of some sixty-five different flies that should be used over a complete fishing year. This was probably the first time anyone recognized that insect activity changed every month, thus requiring a corresponding change in flies for the fly-fisher.

One of the most dramatic advances in equipment occurred with the development of the bamboo rod in 1845. A violin maker in Pennsylvania laminated split segments of bamboo together to create a strong, flexible rod with casting abilities superior to any materials before that time. Bamboo completely changed the methods and process of fly-fishing. Many other changes took place over the years with advances in knowledge and new materials. Even today, with Space Age materials and new conservation methods, these changes and improvements are still going on. Floating fly lines of tapered polyvinyl chloride and Dacron-type core have made silk lines obsolete. Nylon materials have now completely replaced silk gut leaders and tippets. Tomorrow even these materials may become obsolete as improvements continue to be made and with more people fly-fishing today than ever before.

According to some estimates, there are approximately 3 million fly-fishers in the United States today, of whom only a very few are women. Since skill, finesse, and knowledge are the most important requirements for fly-fishing, women often have fewer problems than men learning fly-fishing. This is a surprise to many people, but accuracy and a delicate touch are much more important than upper-body strength. More women are beginning fly-fishing today, but these additions to the fly-fishing congregations (fly-fishing is a form of divine worship for many people) should increase much faster as soon as some of the fog has been lifted. This "fog" has for too long shrouded this splendid art form. This book is intended to clear that fog away. Not the least important of changes that have occurred in recent years has been the addition of women's sizes for the important clothing and equipment, which can enhance the enjoyment of this sport. Everything, from wading boots to fishing vest and hats, is now available in most all women's sizes. In addition, age is no barrier to the beginner. Except for very young children, there is no age limit for starting to fish effectively with a fly rod. Children as young as six years old and senior citizens have started fly-fishing. They are having a lot of fun and satisfaction with this most rewarding form of recreation.

FLY-FISHING
FOR THE
CLUELESS

CHAPTER 1

What Fish Feed On—Insects, Minnows, and Other Things

If a fish kept his mouth shut, he would never get caught; legally, that is. But a fish must eat to survive, and this feeding activity, along with avoiding predators (including man) and reproducing to sustain the species, takes up practically all of its time. That is why understanding the food supply that fish feed on is so important to fly-fishing. As far as food is concerned, trout, bass, bluegill, etc., are almost totally carnivorous. Their diet, for the most part, is made up of crustaceans, worms, insects, other fish, and to a limited extent, some foods classified as plankton and/or certain kinds of vegetation. Artificial flies (a hook with some fur and feathers attached) are imitations of this food, which includes the insects, minnows, and some other types of food that fish feed on.

According to entomologists (scientists who study insects), there are over a million different species of insects here on earth, with almost one hundred thousand living in North America. Fortunately for the angler who is just starting fly-fishing, only the aquatic and a very few terrestrial insects are of concern, since these few insects are the primary source of food for so many fish.

Understanding the fundamental morphology and behavioral characteristics of these insects and their life cycle is extremely important if the right fly is to be selected for presentation to the ever-cautious and suspicious fish. This kind of instruction should not intimidate anyone who is just starting to fish with a fly rod. It is analogous, and similar, to the procedure one would follow when starting to take up any other recreational sport. Remember, this is a sport dedicated to healthy recreation. If you want fish for the table, go to the fish market; the selection is better and cheaper. With any new sport, the best procedure is to first learn the vocabulary, then the rules, the equipment, the configuration of the playing field, and how to keep score, etc. Fly-fishing follows a similar procedure. Just a few basic principles of the science of entomology will give you all the clues you will need to understand which aquatic insects are important to fly-fishing.

Although minnows and small fish are an important part of the fish's diet, especially a larger fish, aquatic insects make up the most important part of a fish's menu. Terrestrial insects, grasshoppers, and ants are also fish food, but they play a relatively minor role in fly-fishing. The exception to this generalization might be the trout, bass, or the bluegill, which will gladly take a grasshopper or cricket any-time it mistakenly falls into the water. This is especially true in late summer. One of the most important characteristics of fish feeding on insects is the manner in which the fish will ingest the insect, either the real one or the fraudulent fly. Unlike the typical bass or saltwater billfish, which will "strike" a lure or live bait, the trout or even the bass feeding on a nymph or insect hatch will inhale or literally suck in the fly. Many times on a trout stream at night this can be heard on the surface of the water as a big "slurp" when there is a hatch. Most importantly, if the fish feels that what he has ingested is artificial or not real, he will spit it out. Many a fly-fisher has failed to set the hook at the right moment and not even noticed that the fly was taken by the fish. Even experienced anglers who have just started fly-fishing have been frustrated by this experience. Understanding how the fish feed and setting the hook properly are the most essential require-ments for fly-fishing in lake or stream. Setting the hook is the act of imbedding the hook in the jaw of the fish before he spits it out. (See chapter 7 for a further explanation of setting the hook.)

The food chain in the water begins with plankton, which is also a generic classification of some plants that convert sunlight into food. They are for the most part macroscopic and microscopic life-forms, such as diatoms and water fleas, that feed on underwa-ter plant life. Most plankton is invisible to the naked eye. Insects and their larvae feed on algae and plankton, and fish feed on in-sects. Most significantly, for the trout family of fishes, insects play the most prominent role in the fish's diet. Along with insects, min-nows and other baitfish make up a big part of the menu of the larger fish. This feeding pattern might also apply to members of the bass family.

Understanding the life cycles of some of the more common aquatic insects is important for fly-fishing, since these insects make up such an important part of food for fish. Even though thousands of insects have thus far been identified, as far as fly-fishing is concerned, only a few of them are significant. Fly-fishermen and fisherwomen have no need to know all of the insect classifications, but they are mentioned here because so many of the charts and announcements of current hatches of aquatic insects will refer to these names along with their local and provincial names. The scientific names of these orders and species are universal and apply everywhere.

All insects are divided into two subclass groups based on the presence or absence of wings. All insects of the class Insecta, which is part of the phylum Arthropoda, can easily be recognized as having six legs and two antennae. The winged insects are of the subclass Apterygota, and this classification is further divided into thirty-one orders, of which five are considered aquatic, at least in their immature, or nymph, stages. As far as fly-fishing is concerned, the most important orders or families of insects for fish food are: Ephemeroptera, or **mayflies;** Plecoptera, or **stone flies;** Trichoptera, or **caddis flies;** and Chironomidae, or nonbiting **midges,** which are all aquatic (see Fig. 1). In addition, the terrestrial insect order of Lepidoptera, or butterflies and moths; Orthoptera, which includes crickets and grasshoppers; and Hymenoptera, which also includes ants, bees, and wasps, are often found on the water (especially late in the summer) and provide excellent food for fish.

Other insect orders that are important, but not as food for fish, are Diptera, or true flies, which include the families of mosquitoes, no-see-ums, blackflies, deerflies, and horseflies (an exception might be the mosquito, which breeds in the water and is a common fish food). These insects are important because they are pests and also carriers of diseases, like the dreaded malaria or yellow fever. Therefore, it is important that the angler use insect repellent and good clothing for protection from these disagreeable insects. Incidentally, one of the most effective malaria-control programs ever devised was by the epidemiologist Pedro Alonso of the University of Barcelona in Spain. After World War II, there was a substantial resurgence of mosquitoes and malaria in Spain. The Spanish

---

Figure 1. Important aquatic flies for fly-fishing

Mayflies *(Ephemeroptera)*

Over 500 Species. The largest is 35 millimeters (1-3/8 inches).

Caddis flies *(Trichoptera)*

Almost 800 Species. Up to 25 millimeters (1 inch).

Stone flies *(Plecoptera)*

Over 400 Species. Up to 50 millimeters (2 inches).

---

stocked their lakes and ponds with a fish called gambusia, which thrives on mosquito larvae. Now Spain has a lot of gambusia but almost no malaria!

Since 90 percent of the aquatic insects consumed by fish are ingested underwater, when the insects are in the egg, larval, or pupal stage, it is important to understand the life cycle of these insects and the factors that influence that cycle.

The life history of the mayfly family of the order Ephemeroptera is typical and certainly one of the most popular. There are something like five hundred species of mayflies in North America, and they occupy almost every kind of freshwater habitat on the continent. There is a considerable variation in the size of these insects, and some of the larger ones in Ireland are even used as live bait on a pole, up to 18 feet long, with a technique called "dapping." There are three "genera" of the Ephemeroptera order. They are:

1. *Ephemera*
2. *Pentagenia*
3. *Hexagenia*

The *Ephemera* genera have three "drake" species that are of interest to the angler. They are:

1. Brown drake (*Ephemera simulans*)
2. Yellow drake (*Ephemera varia*)
3. Eastern green drake (*Ephemera guttulata*)

Pentagenia is an uncommon genus and is most often present in North American rivers with a lot of silt and/or hard clay riverbanks. This genus is seldom copied for an artificial fly. The *Hexagenia* genus has seven known species in North America. The *limbata* species is transcontinental, and the other six species are all east of the continental divide. *Hexagenia limbata* is without a doubt the most popular of the mayflies. It is also the largest mayfly and is known by many local names, some of which are:

1. Great olive-winged drake
2. Great lead-winged drake
3. Michigan caddis (This is really a mayfly. Don't confuse it with a caddis fly, which is a different species.)
4. Giant Michigan mayfly
5. Big yellow maylfly
6. Michigan spinner
7. Burrowing mayfly
8. Sandfly
9. Hex

Mayfly eggs deposited in the water bury themselves in the mud on the bottom of the stream and on the banks and then hatch into the nymph, which spend the fall and winter months feeding on aquatic plants, plankton, etc. The mayfly nymph, *Hexagenia lim-bata,* is well adapted for digging into the mud and can disappear in seconds. Significantly, mayfly nymphs make up one of the largest single food sources for trout and are a major source of food for other fish! Early in the summer, when the nymph reaches maturity, it will struggle to the surface to hatch. At this time, the nymphal skin splits, and the first winged stage emerges. This is the subimago, or dun. This stage is very important in fly-fishing, since the duns now present one of the most attractive meals for the fish. Dry-fly fishing (dry flies float on top of the water) imitating these duns is now at its best. About twenty-four hours later, the skin is shed again, and the fully mature insect emerges into the spinner stage, lifting itself up from the surface of the water or the bank of the stream and rising in the air for mating. Mating of the male and female takes place in the air, usually from 5 to 20 feet above the sur-face of the water. When copulation is complete, both the male and female insects fall to the water, where the female deposits her fer-tilized eggs and the cycle begins all over again. Death comes to both insects very soon after they hit the water. This is the spent spinner stage, and the fish continue their feasting. This entire life cycle may take from one to two years.

Of equal or of even more importance in those waters where they proliferate are the caddis flies. The caddis fly, from the insect order Trichoptera, has almost eight hundred different species in North America and represents a very important source of food for fish. These flies vary in size from less than 1/8 inch in length to as much as 2 inches. Their eggs, deposited in or very near the water, hatch into a wormlike larva, which in most cases then builds a pro-tective case around itself. After about two weeks, the nymph hatches into a winged adult. Most caddis flies are downright drab in appearance. The wings of this insect fold over its body like a tent. In flight it is similar to a moth. The white species of the caddis fly genus *Leptocella* are models for the white miller dry fly. In many streams the caddis is the most important food for trout.

From coast to coast, wherever the water is fast, cold, and with a high oxygen content, the stone fly is one of the most favored foods for trout. The stone flies, order Plecoptera, are represented by nearly four hundred different species and are a major food item for several types of game fish. This insect can only survive in very clean and very fast water. The eggs are deposited by the female underwater, usually at night. After hatching from the egg, the nymphs pass through several molts and after one to two years will hatch into an adult. After crawling from the water and emerging from the nymphal skin, the adult will then rest on nearby trees, rocks, or the shore for several days until the wings harden. Emergence usually occurs at night or early morning. Stone flies are fully winged and at rest fold their wings like a tent over the abdomen. These hatches are very important to the angler, especially when they occur in the spring. These flies become more important as they increase in size. In some parts of the country they can reach 50 millimeters (2 inches) in length. Such a large insect will attract some of the larger trout to the surface that otherwise would remain on the bottom feeding on nymphs or other fish. The stone fly is a perfect food for fish.

The crickets and grasshoppers of the order Orthoptera and ants of the order Hymenoptera are the most common terrestrial order of insects used either as live bait or as artificial flies fished either wet or dry. This food is most popular late in the season, during July, August, and September, when the abundance of these insects spills over into the lakes and streams.

These are the most popular and probably the most common orders of insects that make up the diet of the fish and, of course, the most imitated by the anglers for their artificial flies.

Since mayflies are so common throughout the United States and Canada, some of the most popular dry-fly imitations are described as follows:

1. The Hendrickson is an imitation of the mayfly insect *Ephemerella invaria,* which shows a preference for streams with gravel bottoms where the nymphs can secure adequate anchorage. In Michigan, hatches may start as early as mid-April, when snow is still on the ground, and then reach a peak by the first of May. The trout have a feast when this hatch hits the surface, although the nymphs also provide a bountiful harvest for the fish as they struggle to the surface of the water for the hatch. Other mayfly species, namely, *E. subvaria* and *E. rotunda* are so similar to *E. invaria* that the Hendrickson pattern is also used for these hatches.

2.   The Gray Fox and the Dark Cahill are artificial fly imitations of the mayfly order of Stenonema Vicarium, Stenonema Ithaca, and Stenonema Fuscum. The Gray Fox is used when these mayflies, which are so similar to each other, are still duns, or subimagoes. The colors are mostly brown or yellow-olive, with wings light gray and mottled with dark olive brown. The Dark Cahill is used when they become spinners or full adults. The colors are now dark brown, with the sides of the thorax washed with yellow. The abdomen is brown to amber to yellow near the base. These hatches occur from the middle of May to the middle of July, with the Ithaca starting first, followed by the Fuscum and then the Vicarium. The hatch from nymph to dun usually takes place in late afternoon to early evening. The molt from dun to spinner occurs that same night or early the next morning. Mating starts late that afternoon into the next night at 15–50 feet above the stream. Each of these species does well in large trout streams, not only in cold water but also in warmer water, which might be marginal for trout.

3.   The Olive Dun, *Ephemerella lata,* is a latecomer. This hatch occurs in July and early August, most often after the more abundant mayflies have completed their hatch and reproduction cycle. The dun is nearly black in color, with the legs and wings a bluish black. The spinner is dark brown with white tails and a very dark abdomen. The nymph occurs in three different color phases. One is medium to light brown. The second is dark green, with a collar, the abdominal segments, and gill plates light bluish green. The color of the third phase is more of a green-brown, with stripes ahead of each wing pad and the gills bright red.

4.   The Brown Drake, *Ephemera simulans,* is one of the most important mayflies to inhabit trout streams and lakes. The nymphs burrow in the sand and gravel, and when they rise to the surface for the hatch, the subimago, or dun, is dark brown in color. The wings are olive, with heavy spots of dark brown. These duns usually hatch in the early evening (just after sunset) and provide a rich diet for the feeding trout. The molt from dun to spinner usually takes place later that night or very early the next day. The mating flight then forms the following

evening and/or night, with swarms rising to 5 or 50 feet above the surface of the water. With the range of *E. simulans* from northeastern states to the north-central states, this hatch normally occurs sometime from May 15 to July 10, just before the hatch of the giant *Hexagenia limbata*.

5. The Green Drake, *Ephemera guttulata*, is widely distributed throughout the northeastern United States and Canada. Its habits resemble the Brown Drake, with the dates of the hatch ranging from the middle of May to the middle of June. The most obvious difference between the Brown and the Green is that the abdomen of the Green dun is pale green and in the spinner stage it becomes creamy white, without dark markings. The wings of the Green are more heavily spotted with dark brown than those of the Brown Drake and from a distance appear almost entirely black. Green Drake is the common name given to the dun, but the spinner, or imago, stage is known as the Gray Drake, Black Drake, or even Coffin Fly.

6. Michigan caddis, *Hexagenia limbata*, the largest of the mayflies, is most commonly called the "Michigan caddis," even though this mayfly is not a caddis fly. The nymphs of this species prefer to burrow in the silt and mud bars of the lakes and streams. These nymphs are for the most part amber in color, with the abdomen and the thorax tinted with reddish brown and purple. The gills are purple, with gray edges. The dun is predominantly light green to olive, with the wings olive gray. The spinner has clear wings, and the body color will vary from yellow to dark brown. The tails are longer than the body, but the middle tail is very short.

   This hatch is one of nature's most spectacular fly-fishing shows one could ever witness, and trout are especially appreciative, since they will abandon all caution to feed on this copious supply of insects, sometimes even bumping against the legs of the wading angler while feeding directly in front of the rod and reel. Most often the hatch occurs from the middle of June to the middle of July. Even the larger trout, whose main diet is made up of other fish, will seize this opportunity for a feast. These hatches are sometimes so large (millions and millions) as to present a hazard to automobile traffic when the insects cover the windshield and make the road slippery when they cover the pavement. This problem is most common where the roads are near a stream, especially on the bridges.

When do aquatic insects hatch? Although we know generally when the various hatches occur, we do not know precisely when the dun will reach the surface and when the spinner will rise for the conjugal meetings above the stream. As we know, the entire cycle may be anywhere from one to two years for most of these insects, and the actual hatch is only a very small part of that time, that is, one day or three days, depending on the particular insect. The question is further complicated by the fact that a given hatch may occur along a given stretch of a stream, say for a thousand yards, one night and then appear again the next night a mile downstream. As far as is known, the main triggers for the hatch seem to be temperature and humidity and the proper combination thereof. Fortunately, there is enough experience with these hatches to enable us to formulate tables and charts so that we can estimate with reasonable accuracy when a given hatch will occur. Of course, the most reliable data are from a telephone call to the fishing lodge or sporting-goods store near the stream for any given time or location of a hatch. It's also important to understand that it is the vast numbers of insects in the hatch that attract fish to feed on the surface. This is when the dinner bell is ringing. Even the larger fish don't pass up this invitation. When these hatches do happen and the feeding starts, the only insect the fish will feed on is that particular hatch. No other will do. It's a waste of time to fish a stone fly if a mayfly such as the Brown Drake is hatching.

Other important food sources for fish, especially in lakes and the still waters of large rivers, are leeches, midges, damselflies, freshwater shrimp, and of course, other fish. Of these, the more important are probably the midges, the shrimp, and other fish. Midges, although very small (and the imitation fly is also very small), may swarm over a stream by the millions, and it is not uncommon for fish to gorge themselves on them and even ignore other mayfly hatches on the water. The freshwater species of shrimp are also known as crawfish in the southern coastal regions of the United States. They range from very small to as large as 12 inches in length. They are excellent bait for any fish. The shrimp imitation is fished like a nymph and can attract large fish with the larger imitation fly.

The scud of the order Amphipoda is often called freshwater shrimp. The name is a misnomer, but this shrimplike Amphipoda is one of the most important sources of food for trout and black bass. They vary in size from 1/4 inch to as much as an inch and feed most commonly on aquatic vegetation. Artificial flies imitating shrimp are most effective wherever this type of cover exists in the water.

Other fish or minnows are undoubtedly the main attraction for larger fish. Once a fish gets over 12 inches, other fish are almost certain to be a major part of its diet. The fly hatches and the nymphs just aren't enough. The wet fly or streamer imitations of these preferred foods are one of the best presentations that can be made when fly-fishing. Whether just beginning to fly-fish or after many years of experience, make sure that a good selection of streamers is available for fishing the deep holes and logjams on the lakes and streams.

We know that fish eat foods other than those outlined here. Worms, plankton, ants, mosquitoes, beetles, and even corn and pellets (artificial foods), just to name a few, but the foods listed here are of primary interest to anyone who is beginning fly-fishing. Understanding these food sources makes fly-fishing that much easier and more enjoyable. Next, check the following chart (Fig. 2) for the time of year when the various hatches occur at your favorite fly-fishing lake or stream. As everyone knows, the best time to go fishing is whenever you can. When this blessing occurs and you know your fishing location, use the chart and be prepared for that particular hatch. Of course, don't ever forget that even though a particular hatch isn't taking place when you are at your favorite fishing hole, the fish still have to eat, and your wet flies, nymphs, and streamers are the best bet until the hatch starts. With few exceptions, the big fish won't start feeding at the surface on a particular hatch until the large swarms begin the hatching ritual. Remember that quantity of the insect hatch is just as important to the fish as the particular insect the fish prefer at that time.

It's also important to remember that stream and lake conditions determine to a considerable extent the predominant aquatic fly and its nymphs in that part of the lake or stream. Mayflies generally will predominate in those parts of the lake or stream with muddy bottoms and/or muddy banks. Caddis flies prefer sandy bottoms and/or banks, and stone flies prefer very fast water with sand and gravel bottoms. These are generalizations, of course, but if the angler can take time to study the stream conditions as well as the hatching charts, a better estimate can be made for the proper fly selection.

Saltwater fish feed under the surface of the water most of the time. As far as fly-fishing is concerned, the primary foods for these fish are shrimp, crabs, and baitfish. The tides have the biggest influence on the availability of this food supply for the saltwater fish in any of the coastal waters. The current created by the tides moves the food for the fish to feed on. In between tides, with the high-water slack or the low-water slack and no movement of the water, the food is harder for the fish to find. Steamer flies, crab patterns, shrimp patterns, and poppers imitating these different food choices make up most of the flies in the tackle box for saltwater fly-fishing.

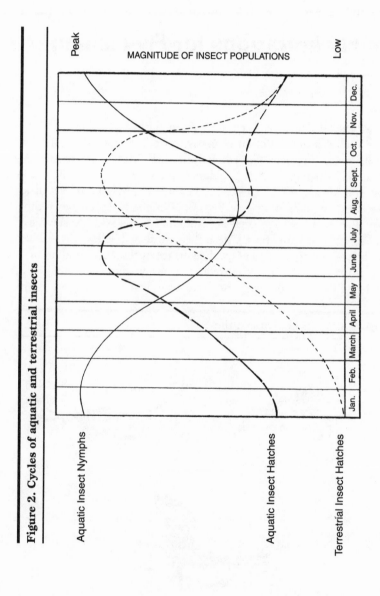

Figure 2. Cycles of aquatic and terrestrial insects

CHAPTER 2

Fly Imitations for Fly-Fishing

The term "fly," as used in fly-fishing, is a generic term and includes the imitation of many more fish foods than just insects. Artificial flies can imitate such fish foods as minnows, sculpins, shrimp, leeches, spiders, and even worms and crustaceans. Most artificial flies can be classified as nymphs or wet flies, dry flies, and streamers (see Fig. 3). Nymphs and wet flies represent the immature life stages of aquatic insects such as mayflies, caddis flies, or stone flies. These flies are fished below the surface of the water. Dry flies float on the surface of the water and imitate the adult stages of aquatic insects that are at the end of their life cycle, ready to reproduce, or terrestrial insects that have been

Figure 3. Types of artificial flies

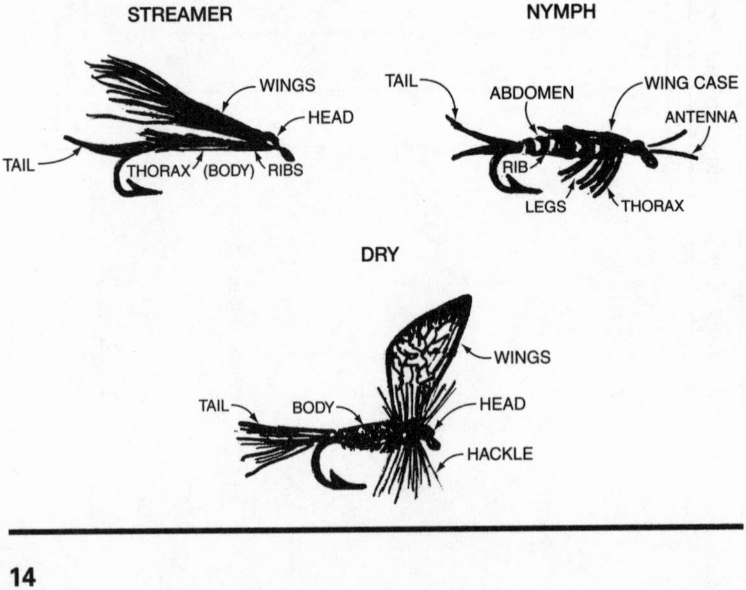

STREAMER

WINGS
HEAD
TAIL
THORAX (BODY) RIBS

NYMPH

TAIL
ABDOMEN
WING CASE
ANTENNA
RIB
LEGS
THORAX

DRY

TAIL
BODY
WINGS
HEAD
HACKLE

blown onto the water by the wind, such as grasshoppers, ants, or crickets. Bass bugs and poppers are also dry flies, since they float on the surface and are very good artificial baits for bass and panfish. Streamers are the flies that imitate minnows, sculpins, leeches, and/or shrimp. Streamers represent a large food supply for fish and are especially known for their ability to take large fish.

Fly sizes are referred to by a number that identifies the size of the hook on which the fly is tied. Hook sizes are determined by shank length, not including the eye. The fly-size (hook-size) range for most fly-fishing is from No. 20 to 2/0, although hook sizes may range from as small as No. 32 to as large as 22/0. Trout flies are therefore numbered, with the smallest hook size having the largest number. For example, a size 18 brown drake is smaller than a size 12 brown drake. Very large hook sizes are identified with a zero (0) added to the hook number, for example, 1/0. For these large hooks, the larger the number in front of the virgule, the larger the hook; 5/0 is larger than 1/0. For any hook size, the length of the hook shank can be standard, extra long (XL), or extra short (XS).

The following table illustrates the sizes of the most commonly used hooks (flies) for fly-fishing.

Size No.	Length (inches)	Wire Diameter (inches)
2/0	1 5/8	.045
1/0	1 1/2	.043
1 1/2	1 3/8	.041
1	1 1/4	.039
2	1 1/8	.037
4	15/16	.033
6	13/16	.030
9	11/16	.027
10	9/16	.024
12	7/16	.021
14	11/32	.018
16	9/32	.016
18	7/32	.014
20	5/32	.012

Variations from these standards are made for special flies. For example, streamer hooks for long, slender flies, which represent minnows, are shown as 2X long or 3X long. That is, two or three sizes longer than the standard shank length. Heavy hooks may be shown as 2X stout or 3X stout. That is, two or three sizes heavier than the standard wire diameter. Lighter hooks, for dry fly-fishing, are 2X fine or 3X fine.

When you are about to start fly-fishing, it is very important to find out what the fish are feeding on at that particular time of day or night or time of year before you select a particular artificial fly to present to the fish. Since there is considerable variation in the diet of the fish from day to day or from hour to hour and the variation of the insects for the food supply is very great, only careful observation will tell you what the feeding pattern is for a particular time. Because of the great differences in size for any order of the insects, for example, Ephemeridae mayflies, of which there are something like five hundred, the size of the different species can vary from as small as 4 millimeters (1/8 inch), say a No. 20 hook, up to 38 millimeters or 1 1/2 inches, say a No. 1/0 hook, for the giant Michigan *Hexagenia limbata*. About the only sure way one can tell what particular hatch is swarming is to catch one with your hands and look at it. This simple tactic will help avoid much frustration and empty creels.

Matching the hatch is an imperative for the dry-fly angler; and if there is no hatch, a good estimate of what nymph or streamer to use is needed to tempt the feeding fish. Trial and error may eventually put some "fish on" the line, but success will come much faster if the angler can discover what hatch is taking place and then select the proper fly to match. Anglers have debated for years the relative importance of size, color, and shape, or profile, of the fly imitation to present to the fish. In recent years the significance of color seems to be discounted more and more by the experts (except for salmon flies), and the size and profile are emphasized more for a successful match of the hatch. In this regard, please remember that many fly imitations, such as an Adams, can come in sizes ranging from a No. 14 hook, almost 9 millimeters, or nearly 3/8 inch long, to a 6 hook, about 20 millimeters, or 13/16 inch long. Most schedules of fly hatches will offer some indication of what size fly (hook) the imitation should be to match the scheduled hatch. When the first fish is caught, check the stomach contents to make sure of the flies that the fish are feeding on at that time. There is also a small stomach pump available to make this inspection simpler.

The number of fly patterns illustrated in the abundance of literature today can be very intimidating to the fly-fishing beginner. Knowing all of them is certainly not necessary to start fly-fishing. A basic selection of flies that should be adequate for the beginning angler might include the following. (Note the various-size hooks recommended so that the proper size can be selected to match the size of the hatch at the time.)

Dry Flies (by hook size)

Adams Nos. 10, 14, 18, and 20, for a total of 4
Hendrickson Nos. 12 and 14, for a total of 2
Red Quill No. 14, for a total of 1
Olive Caddis Nos. 12 and 16, for a total of 2
Olive Winged Drake Nos. 6 and 8, for a total of 2
Royal Coachman Nos. 12 and 16, for a total of 2

Nymphs

Yellow Stone Fly Nos. 12 and 16, for a total of 2
Hendrickson Nos. 14 and 16, for a total of 2
Brown Drake No. 12, for a total of 1
Great Olive Winged Drake or the Michigan Hex, also called
    Clark Lynn Nymph Nos. 6 and 8, for a total of 2
Big Golden Stone Fly Nos. 6 and 8, for a total of 2
White Miller Nos. 12, 14, and 16, for a total of 3
Black Wooly Worm Nos. 8, 12, and 14, for a total of 3

Streamers and Bucktails

Muddler Minnow Nos. 4, 8, and 12, for a total of 3
Black Wooly Bugger Nos. 2, 6, and 8, for a total of 3

Terrestrials

Black Ant Nos. 14 and 18, for a total of 2
Henderson Hopper Nos. 8 and 12, for a total of 2

This is a general guide only. When in a strange fishing area, the angler should check with the local fly shops for the latest information on stream conditions, hatches, etc. The thirty-eight flies of different sizes listed here should cover most of the situations for most of the time in the eastern and midwestern part of the United States. A comparable list for the western part of the country would not be very much different for the beginner. Although these thirty or forty flies cover a broad spectrum of what might be expected on any given lake or stream, it is still too much to expect any angler, especially the beginner, to have all of these available in the middle of a stream or lake when one starts to fish. I believe that the best selection that the angler can carry in the fly wallet, whenever the opportunity to fish is available, would be as follows:

1. The Adams with at least two sizes, namely, Nos. 10 and 18. (dry)
2. The Hendrickson, No. 12. (dry)
3. The Olive Caddis, No. 12. (dry)
4. The Royal Coachman, No. 12 (dry)
5. Yellow Stone, Nos. 12 and 16 (nymph)
6. Olive Winged Drake or the Clark Lynn Nymph, No. 6 (nymph)
7. Black Wooly Worm, Nos. 8 or 12 (nymph)
8. Muddler Minnow, Nos. 8 or 10 (streamer)
9. Black Marabou, Nos. 6 or 8 (streamer)
10. Black Ant, No. 14 (terrestrial)
11. Henderson Hopper, No. 12 (terrestrial)

This short list of sixteen flies will cover the broadest range of conditions. They are very standard because they are flies that consistently catch fish under most circumstances.

Remember, the critical measurement is for the size (note the different sizes for the same fly), the shape or profile, and last of all, the color. As soon as the neophyte accumulates some experience in a given stream or area, the list can easily be modified to accommodate the local conditions. Remember also that the fish will sooner or later destroy a favorite fly and it will have to be replaced. After each strike, examine the fly closely for such damage.

Fully equipped with an arsenal of flies like the ones listed above, the angler is now ready to begin fishing with the fraudulent flies for the ever-wary trout, bass, or panfish. But what fly selection to make for a start? Having checked most of the basics, for example, water temperature, time of day, direction of the wind, and whether or not the cows in the pasture that day were spread out or huddled together, trial and error, starting with the prettiest-color fly in the box just might tempt a fish for that first strike. Note, cows huddled together in the pasture usually means low atmospheric pressure, foretelling a storm. Cows scattered in the pasture mean a high-pressure atmosphere and good fishing. A more reliable guide, however, would be to check the emergence schedule for the flies that inhabit your particular stream, river, or lake as well as the local weather forecast. Remember also that even though the schedule shows a particular hatch occurring at the time you are fishing, hatches occur sporadically along stretches of river or parts of a lake. A brown drake hatch may emerge along two or three miles of a stream one night and then make its appearance downstream (or upstream), five miles away from the previous hatch the next night. To zero in on what is really going on in the area where you are going to fish, check with the local fly shop, or better yet, with someone who just fished there the day before.

Many of these points of caution are just taken for granted by the angler with a lot of experience in fly-fishing, especially fishing a particular part of the stream or lake in which you might be interested. For the beginner, following a good set of guidelines will help success come a lot faster. Like any other sport, most of this will soon become second nature. *The Emergence Schedule,* which is published for different regions of the country, is probably one of the best guides ever made available for the angler who is fly-fishing. Although many variables can alter the precise start of a hatch, for example, temperature, humidity, atmospheric pressure, etc., the life cycles of the insect world comply very closely to a predictable pattern of producing eggs, larvae (nymphs), and finally, hatches. Because entomologists have taught us something about these insects and their cycles, these emergence schedules can be compiled, and the angler can get some idea of what to expect on the water for a given time of the year. The following Midwest schedule is typical for most parts of the country:

Midwestern Fly Hatches and Their Imitations

Common Name	Scientific Name	Emergence	Description	Matching Imitation
Early stone flies	The order is Pleceoptera	3/15–5/5	body dark brown	Early Stone No. 14 dry
Black stone fly	*Taeniopteryx nivalis*	midday	wings, medium gray	Nymph No. 14 wet
Brown stone fly	*Brachyptera fasciata*	midday	wings, dark brown	Early Stone No. 14 dry
Blue wing olive	*Ephemeridae baetidae vagan*	4/15–8/25, noon to dusk	black body wings, slate gray	Iron Dun Nos. 18–20
Black midge	Chironomidae	5/1–5/20, late mornings	body dark blue gray wings gray upright	Black Midge Nos. 18–20 wet
Yellow drake mayfly	*Ephemerella invaria*	5/1–5/20, afternoon to evenings	male, reddish brown female, cream gray	Hendrickson Nos. 12–14 dry Adams No. 14 dry Red Quill No. 14
Little caddis	The order is Trichoptera	4/15–9/1	drab gray wings fold like a tent	White Miller No. 12

(table continued on next page)

(table continued from previous page)

Common Name	Scientific Name	Emergence	Description	Matching Imitation
Dark cahill or sand drake	*Stenoma vicarium, ithaca,* and *fuscum*	5/15–7/15, evenings	body amber-brown rings wings gray, mottled	Gray Fox Nos. 12–14 dry
Green drake mayfly	*Ephemera guttulata*	5/20–6/15	gray-olive wings	Green Drake No. 12 dry Green Adams Nos. 12–14
Brown drake	*Ephemera simulans*	5/15–7/10; best hatch is after midnight	dark brown spots on wings	Brown Drake No. 12 about 7–10 days before Hex. Limbata hatch
Great olive-winged hex hatch or Great drake mayfly	*Ephemeridae hexagenia limbata*	6/15–7/20, evening 8:30–12:00	gray wings and yellow body	Olive Winged Drake No. 8
Light cahill	*Ephemeroptera stenomena*	6/15–8/10, afternoon	yellow wings, orange body	Cahill No. 12
White miller	*Ephemeroptera ephoron album*	8/15–9/15 dusk	white wings, white body	White Miller Nos. 12–14
Ants, grasshoppers	Terrestrials	all summer, daytime	Ants, black; hoppers, brown	Black ant No. 18 Henderson Hopper Nos. 8–12

This schedule is only an illustration for the angler who is just starting to fly-fish. It certainly does not include all of the aquatic and terrestrial insect hatches that occur during the year, but it should help the neophyte who is fishing anywhere in the United States, from the Appalachians to the Rockies. For more extensive listings and detailed emergence schedules, the beginner should consult local fish hatcheries and fly-fishing clubs, which are usually very generous with such information as soon as it is available.

FISHING DRY FLIES

Without a doubt, fishing with dry flies is the most popular method of fly-fishing. The reason for its popularity is because it is nearly 100 percent visual. The fly-fisher can watch the fly on the surface of the water and then watch the fish take it while he sets the hook. It is by far one of the most exciting ways to catch trout, panfish, bass, and many saltwater species. Dry-fly fishing is fishing with a fly that floats on the surface of the water. Dry flies are recognized by the amount of hackle (chicken-neck feathers) and wings tied near the head of the fly. These flies are generally tied from naturally buoyant materials, and to facilitate flotation, they are constructed with very light wire hooks treated with a silicon ointment. It is important that the hackle along with the wings and the rest of the fly be sprayed with a floatation material to be sure that the fly will float on the water. Dry-fly fishing is easier than fishing with streamers, wet flies, or nymphs. However, it does require more care and accuracy than fishing flies underwater, and of course, the fly line must be a floating line. Since many fish in streams and some lakes face upstream to catch the food that the current brings to them, it is important that the dry fly be presented in a manner that will allow it to float naturally over the fish's cone of vision for a strike. A poor cast will not only put the fly where the fish cannot see it but may well spook the fish when the line hits the water too close to the holding area of the fish.

If the fly-fisher can see that the fish are feeding on the surface, the target for presenting the dry fly can be selected so that the fly will pass directly over the feeding fish. In many cases this will mean casting the fly upstream and/or up and across the stream for the right presentation. It is most important that the fly floats and moves naturally on the surface of the water. Any unnatural drag on the line from a poor cast or from the floating line moving faster than the fly and leader will spook the fish. As the fly begins to float downstream, you should immediately begin the retrieve or to strip (recover the line by hand) in the surplus line with your line hand so that when a fish strikes you can set the hook right away. When retrieving the line with your line hand, run the line over the index finger of your rod hand for the best control of the line. Also remember, after the fly enters the fish's window of vision, the fish may follow it for some distance. This whole process may be repeated several times before the fish actually takes the fraudulent fly. Whether the presentation is made upstream or upstream and across, this method is one of the best for fishing the dry fly.

Where the water doesn't move much, as in lakes and mill ponds, present your dry fly to the most likely spot for the trout, bass, or panfish and let the fly sit for a few moments. In still waters, fish cruise around in search of their food, as contrasted with fish in a stream, which usually lie waiting for the currents to bring the food to them. Panfish and bass like to pounce on their food, and they prefer to see some movement that indicates that the quarry is alive and good to eat. Therefore, when the fly is sitting for a few moments, give it a twitch or a jig. The movement with the noise will attract the fish and encourage them to take the fly. A very old technique used for fishing for bass and/or panfish is to use a small popper with a nymph or streamer dropper (additional fly usually fastened to the leader) attached to the bend of the hook with a short piece of tippet material.

FISHING STREAMERS

Although most fly-fishers might express a preference for fishing a "hatch" on any given lake or stream, in fact, most of the bigger fish will be caught on a wet fly or a streamer. Streamers, of course, imitate small fish, not insects. Small fish, or baitfish, as they are often called, are the mainstay diet for the larger freshwater and saltwater fish. If you can cast your line out only 20 feet, you can catch fish in streams and lakes with a streamer. Just lay the streamer out on the water and let it drift with the current naturally. The line and the streamer itself will swim the fly so that it looks like a swimming baitfish or a wounded minnow. Even fish that are not hungry will strike a wounded minnow. If there is no hatch when you are fishing your favorite lake or stream, try a streamer like a Wooly Bugger. Cast into the current and be ready for that first strike. Don't forget to use some strike putty or yarn (attached to the line so you can see the line dip below the water) to help you with this attractive fly. If you suspect that you are not fishing at the right holding level for the fish, add some split shot (small lead pellets) about 3–15 inches above the fly to sink the streamer to where the fish is. Give the rod tip a bounce now and then as the streamer drifts downstream. This will cause the streamer to jig up and down like a wounded minnow. Most strikes will occur just after the bounce when the fly is free-falling in the current. Do your best to select the streamer that you suspect will imitate the food the fish are feeding on. Either a Clouser Minnow, Muddler Minnow, or a Zonker, along with the Wooly Bugger, make up an excellent addition to the selection. If fishing the streamer in a lake where there is no current, you will have to swim the fly along with an occasional jig and/or twitch to imitate a wounded baitfish. In a stream, cast across the current. In a boat, cast toward the shore and retrieve fast, then slow.

FISHING NYMPHS

If the fish just are not feeding at the surface of the water, they are feeding below the surface. Nymphs are by far one of the favorite underwater food sources for fish. The artificial fly imitating the immature insect must be employed with the same care and casting accuracy as the dry fly. The size of the fly should match the size of the tippet and the leader and of course the weight of the fly line and the rod. The same rod and line used for fishing dry flies can be used for fishing nymphs. An 8–8 1/2-foot rod with a 5- or 6-weight line can serve dry flies, wet flies, and streamers very well for the neophyte. In any case, the leader and tippet should not be longer than the rod. A 4X, 5X, or 6X should be adequate for most of the fishing. Be sure to stock up with a good supply of strike indicators (red yarn or yellow putty) and split-shot sinker weights. Adjusting the weight on the leader for each fishing situation is a key to catching good fish on nymphs.

Fishing the nymph is really short-line fishing. A cast of 30 feet is many times too long. Short casts are the rule. Cast up and across, working the fly on a slow drift through the pockets of water holding the fish. Hold the rod up at about a 45-degree angle as the nymph moves with the current in front of you. Hold as much of the line up out of the water as possible and watch the strike indicator. Fast control of your line is very important. Usually the fish will hit the nymph as it hits the water. Too many neophytes miss their strikes because they don't have control of the line and don't see the strikes as they happen. Stop your cast with the rod tip low to the water and raise it smoothly to pick up the slack line. Control the excess slack by moving the rod to the side as your fly (nymph) moves downstream with the currents. If the water current is faster and you need to strip line to keep things under control, place the line under the index finger of your rod hand just before the fly hits the water on the forward cast. Immediately take a few strips and remove the initial slack while you raise the rod and follow the line across and downstream. On cast, where you can control the slack by just raising your rod, you are ready to set the hook immediately when you see your line or indicator change direction in relation to the current. Select the right amount of split-shot weight to add to your leader for each pocket or pool of water that you fish. Adjust this weight for each fishing situation. Put the weight just above the tippet part of your leader about 15–18 inches above your fly. A tippet that is too long can result in missed strikes. Fish can spit out a fraudulent fly very fast, and even a little slack in your tippet will give the fish a chance to pick up and spit out your nymph before you detect a strike. Most of the time you need to get your nymph close to the bottom as soon as possible, but in any event, the nymph should look lifelike and drift freely with the currents for the fish.

For most pocket-water fishing, fish upstream, working the pockets either across or up and across. Do your best not to spook (frighten) the fish with your movements in the stream or lake bottom by kicking up too much mud and/or noise.

CHAPTER 3

Fly-Fishing Tackle

For an angler starting to fly-fish, a fundamental selection of equipment is needed to learn how to fish with a fly rod. Although equipment is necessary for the sport, do not buy any of this important gear to start fly-fishing. Either borrow or rent the equipment to learn some of the important techniques, or better yet, take some lessons in fly-fishing from a school where the equipment is supplied for the course. It is not just the expense involved, although that can be a substantial amount, but most of the equipment is very personal. For example, a No. 6 rod might be just right for me for fishing panfish and trout, but a No. 5 or even a No. 4 rod might be best for you to do the same kind of fishing. This same kind of rationale could apply to the fly line, the leaders, and even the tippets. As far as expense is concerned, it should be remembered that like so much athletic equipment, most of the available fishing tackle exceeds the ability of most people to use it. A moderately priced outfit will last anyone a lifetime with reasonable care. A basic fly-fishing rig will also provide a sound foundation from which to expand to more elaborate assemblies that might be needed for saltwater fishing or steelhead fishing. The best way to start, however, is to keep the tackle assembly as simple as possible. For most people and for most of the fishing situations the angler will encounter, the following equipment and how to choose it should be adequate to start fly-fishing:

THE FLY ROD

If you haven't a clue about fly-fishing, especially if you have never even fished before, it's important to understand how to choose a fly rod for the kind of fishing you are going to do; for example, panfish, bass, trout, saltwater fish, etc. Notwithstanding the fact that you may be starting out with some rented equipment or even some hand-me-down equipment, at least you should understand what that equipment can and cannot do. Fly-fishers do more casting with their fly rods than any other kind of fishing. For this reason if for no other, the weight of the rod becomes more important. For some rods, the longer you cast with them, the heavier they become. There is no one-size-fits-all fly rod, but rods can be selected that will be the most helpful to learn fly-casting and still satisfy most of your fly-fishing needs. The very first consideration in choosing a fly rod (hand-me-down or brand-new) is to find the proper line weight for the kind of fishing you will do. The size of the rod you select should match the weight of the line as closely as possible. In other words, a No. 6 rod is built for a No. 6 line. Most important, the line weight determines the size of the fly you can cast accurately, which indicates the size of fish you are after.

Line weights come in sizes 1–14, with one being the lightest. Lighter lines are obviously used for smaller fish in smaller bodies of water. Conversely, when fishing large lakes, rivers, and especially salt water, you would want to cast larger flies with a heavier line. As an example, if you will be fishing for panfish and small trout, a No. 3 line weight would be about right. If you will be fishing for trout on a large stream or bass on a warm-water lake, a line weight of No. 5 or even No. 7 might be the right selection. For heavier fish like steelhead or saltwater fish like redfish or snook, a No. 8 line would be about the right selection. To find the weight of the line to match the rod, look for the third number in a rod name on the newer rods. For example a number of 85-6F indicates a rod length of 8 feet 6 inches for a No. 6 floating line. In other words, this would be a 6-weight rod.

The next important choice is for the length of the rod. Here the choice of length would depend on where you are going to fish. For small streams with overhanging bushes, a short rod would be the choice for more control. For larger streams and salt water, a longer rod would be more helpful for casting longer distances and mending (correcting the sag of the line on the water) the line after the cast. To find the rod length, look at the first two numbers on the rod. For a number 85-6F, the first two numbers, 85, indicate a

rod 8 feet 6 inches long. For the beginner, a medium-action fly rod
7–8 1/2 feet in length for a 5-weight line is a good choice. These
rods can be made of split bamboo, compounds of graphite, or fiberglass. The least expensive of these is fiberglass. Glass fiber is probably the strongest of the fly-rod materials, but the glass fiber
strands must be held together by a strong laminating agent. It is
this bonding glue that comes apart with too much use or abuse.
Thus fiberglass rods are only as good as the glue used to hold them
together. No matter, fiberglass is still one of the most economical
fly rods for the neophyte fly-fisher. The rods made up of compounds of graphite, although much lighter weight, are more expensive. Some of these can cost hundreds, even thousands, of dollars.
However, in recent years, the compound rod made of a combination of fiberglass and graphite has reduced the price considerably.
The compound rod with more graphite in its composition is more
expensive. Bamboo rods, which are heavier, are also more expensive, since most of them are handmade. For the beginner, get the
best you can afford. Superior equipment always makes learning
easier. Most important, get a good sturdy case for the rod at the
same time you buy the rod. Most damage to fly rods comes from
automobile doors, luggage handlers, closet doors, etc. Fly rods
come in either two or four sections. The two-section rods are standard and are usually less expensive than the four-section rods. In
addition, since practically all rods come in sections, try to purchase an extra tip, especially if you're going to fish at some remote
location. Broken tips are undoubtedly the most common accidents
that occur with fly rods.

Fly rods are also classified according to the amount of their
"flex," or the amount that they bend from the inertial forces generated with either a backcast or a forward cast. In other words, when
the rod is brought back with a backcast up to the 11 o'clock position
on the clock scale, the momentum of the weight of the rod will continue to force (bend) the rod in a backward motion, even though
the motion of the rod has been stopped at the rod handle by the angler. Depending on the length of the rod, the distribution of its
weight, which will determine where its center of gravity is, and the
material of the rod, which will determine how stiff it is, this extended motion will be at a maximum with a full flex (complete

bending from the rod handle), otherwise known as a slow action; or a mid-flex called medium action, where most of the bending occurs at the midsection of the rod; or a very stiff motion, called a fast-action rod. For a fast-action rod, most all of the bending occurs at the tip of the rod.

A slow-action, full-flex rod bends throughout its length. It acts like a long leaf spring (a spring made of steel strips). During the backcast the rod stores energy from the casting motion. When the backcasting motion is stopped, the rod continues to bend from its momentum and then will spring forward, releasing its stored-up energy. A full-flex rod will be easier on your muscles, but it doesn't have the strength of the fast-action rods.

A medium-action, mid-flex rod provides the best performance over the widest range of conditions and different casting techniques. This type of rod is highly recommended for the beginner. The fast-action rod, or tip-flex rod, is more for advanced casters. It acts more like a lever than a leaf spring, with only the tip of the rod generating much flex on the backcast. This rod requires more skill for accurate casting.

It should be emphasized that the flexibility (flex) of a rod is proportionate to its length as well as the material it is made from. The longer the rod, the more flexibility and the ability to make a longer cast with more accuracy. When fishing from a boat, the longer rod will pick up more line and keep your backcast high. Short rods tend to be a little stiffer and faster, and they give you more control on small streams. Short rods are better for small streams and pond situations, and long rods are better for larger streams and lakes.

Reel seats for fly rods are almost always located below the grip of the rod so that the reel will not interfere with the casting of the fly line. An aluminum or plastic hood and a threaded locking ring are usually used to secure the reel to the rod at the reel seat.

Fly rods today are almost always identified with the length, weight, and line weight imprinted on either the butt cap, next to the reel seat at the bottom of the rod, or on the butt section of the rod just above the hook keeper. A specification might be written: "Eagle (by Fenwick), 8 feet 6 inches, No. 6 line, 3 ounces."

Figure 4. Fly rod and parts

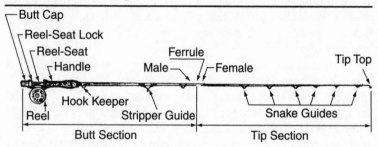

Fly-rod materials are either fiberglass, bamboo, or graphite.
Fly-rod handles are usually made of cork.
Fly-rod hardware is usually aluminum.
Fly-rod reels are either single action with clicker drag to avoid backlash or
    heavier adjustable drag for bigger fish; or automatic retrieve.

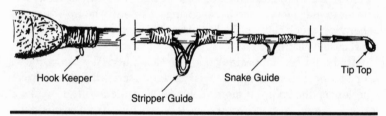

THE REEL

Based on the evidence of a painting by the celebrated Chinese artist
Ma Yuan, the reel was known as long ago as the early thirteenth
century. It has been suggested that the reel was patterned after the
early use of the bobbin in the silk industry. Many experts used to believe that the reel was unimportant, since all it does is provide a storage place for the line. For the smaller fish, up to 1 or even 2 pounds,
this is probably true, since the flexing action of the rod is sufficient
to tire the fish out and enable the angler to put him into the net.
However, the action or procedure is different for a fish over 2
pounds. Once a large fish has taken the fly and the hook is set, it is
very important that the fish be allowed to "run" so that he doesn't
snap the leader or tear the hook from his mouth. Once the pull on

Figure 5. Fly-rod actions

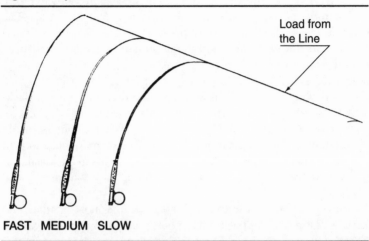

Load from
the Line

FAST MEDIUM SLOW

the line by the fish exceeds the capacity of the rod to bend, the angler should simply allow the fish to run more line from the reel with the drag set. The drag on a reel is analogous to the brake on a car. It is a mechanism to slow down the revolutions of the reel by some means of frictional resistance. On a car, this is accomplished by either brake shoes or disk. On a reel, it is accomplished by different methods, such as a clicker, the most simple drag, which will help avoid a reel backlash (snarl of the line on the reel) or a sophisticated disk arrangement built into the reel to "slow" down the reel revolutions and to provide increased resistance to the pull on the line by a big fish. Drag doesn't stop the reel from revolving; it just makes it more difficult for the fish to pull the line off from the reel. This resistance along with the stiffness of the rod to resist bending is what tires the fish out. Remember, if the drag is set too tight, the fish will snap the line or the leader with his run. To accomplish this strategy of tiring the fish out before you land him, all of the line and backing you have available on the reel must be at the disposal of the fish. Any attempt to horse (yank) the fish in will inevitably mean a loss of the fish, since the leader and tippet only have a strength of 2, 4, 6, or 10 pounds; and if the fish weighs anywhere from 1 pound to as much as 10 pounds, it could easily snap the line with a sudden jerk or thrust as it tries to throw the hook. This is especially true for such larger fish as the steelhead, salmon, and many saltwater fish, which under normal conditions may run from 15 to 20 pounds. The solution to this problem is to set the drag on the reel just right and let the fish run with this continuous pressure until he is too tired to resist any longer. Good reels have adjustable drags that can be adjusted for the kind of fish you expect to catch. The bigger the fish, the more drag is needed. In addition, the drag helps avoid backlash when stripping line from the reel while casting. An adjustable drag, of course, adds to the expense of a reel but is highly recommended for the beginner as well as the experienced angler. A simple "clicker" drag is all that's required to avoid backlash, but if you can afford it, buy the adjustable drag. You will not be disappointed.

Single-action (not automatic) reels are the most popular and have a distinct advantage: The spools that hold the line can be changed very easily. In addition to this advantage, the interchangeability of many reel spools in the reel housing will permit right- or left-hand winding of the crank handle according to the preference of the angler. This flexibility also allows the angler to change to different weights of fishing line by merely changing the spool of the reel. Finally, always put the adhesive label "Fly Line Marker" on the reel spool so you will always know what weight line is on the spool. Automatic reels don't have this convenient flexibility. Automatic reels, although preferred by some experienced anglers, are not recommended for beginners. The instant response in touching the button to rewind the reel can be disastrous.

The capacity of the reel, or any spare spool for the reel, should be carefully checked for the line that the reel spool is to carry. Remember, the reel, as well as any additional spool, must not only carry the line but also the backing for the line. Backing is extra line attached to the fly line to provide for additional line capacity when a big fish makes a run for it and more line is needed than the normal length of fly line. Backing is usually made of braided nylon and is not as expensive as the fly line. It's a good idea to purchase the reel, fly line, and backing at the same time to make sure they are all compatible. First, wind the fly line (about 90 feet) on the reel spool. Then wind the backing onto the reel on top of the fly line until about a half-inch of space is left from the edge of the reel and the lines wound on the reel. After this test, remove the lines from the reel and then reverse the procedure. Fasten the backing line onto the arbor of the spool first, then splice the fly line to the backing and wind the line onto the reel. The total amount of the lines on the reel will vary for the sizes of rod, reel, fly line, and backing. For example, an 8-foot-6-inch 3-ounce 6F rod with a Martin Model 67N reel (with a 2 5/8-inch spool), a DT6F fly line (30 yards), and 75–100 yards of braided backing are typical for trout and freshwater fishing. Larger rods, bigger reels, and heavier lines are needed for bigger fish, for example, steelhead, salmon, and larger saltwater fish.

FLY LINES

To properly select a fly line for the rod and reel, it is helpful to first understand the casting problem. As we all know, what is being cast is the fly line, not the fly at the end of the line. To make a good cast, the line on the backcast, as well as the forward cast, should remain level and parallel to the surface of the water. This is necessary so that a proper loop can be formed and then extended to complete the cast and place the fly on the target. If the line is too heavy for the rod, the extended line on the backcast and forward cast will form a sag or belly in the air and hit the water before the leader and the fly. If the line matches the rod, there should be no sag in the air, and the extended line will turn over smoothly, keeping the weight portion of the line off the water until the cast is completed. Most important, the distribution of that weight and matching that weight to the fly rod are fundamental considerations in selection of a fly line.

The early fly lines were made of braided horsehair, then silk. Today's lines are made of improved nylon with coatings of polyvinyl chloride, which not only have uniform weight distribution but also perform with superb consistency. To eliminate much of the confusion that used to frustrate anglers about the choice of a fly line, the American Fishing Tackle Manufacturers Association (AFTMA) established standards for the manufacture and sale of fly lines that make the choice much easier today.

The following standards apply to practically all new fly lines produced today:

AFTMA Standards for Fly Lines		
No.	**Weight (grains)**	**Symbols**
1	60	L = Level
2	80	DT = Double Taper
3	100	WF = Weight Forward
4	120	ST = Single Taper
5	140	Types
6	160	F = Floating
7	185	S = Sinking
8	210	I = Intermediate (Float/Sink)
9	240	
10	280	
11	330	
12	380	

Note: These weights are based on the first 30 feet of line, not including the taper. It should also be noted that 437 1/2 grains = 1 ounce and 7,000 grains = 1 pound.

Most neophytes ask the question "Why are there so many fly lines?" The answer is that each line is designed for a specific fishing job. One doesn't use a particular line for a 2-pound brook trout and then use that same line for a 10-pound steelhead or a 40-pound saltwater tarpon. A properly selected line will do a better job in getting your fly to the specific target than will any other line. As the beginner gains experience, the need for different lines will become more and more apparent. If you are just starting fly-fishing, use a floating weight-forward line first; but when you discover that 90 percent of the time fish feed below the surface, other lines become important, too. When you choose your fly line, there are three criteria used to make the choice: line weight, line function (floating, sinking, etc.), and finally, the taper of the line from the relatively thick butt end to the tippet at the end of the line.

Today line weights range from 1 weight to 14 weight. Weights 1–12 are the most common, as indicated on the chart. The lighter lines are used for very small flies, and the heavier lines can cast larger flies for longer distances even in windy conditions. Most important, the weight of the line should be compatible with the rod. As noted before, rods today are usually marked with the weight number of the line for the rod on the butt cap or on the rod just above the hook keeper.

Line Weights

Nos. 3 and 4 weight-forward lines probably provide the best opportunity for a delicate presentation to the fish. The very low weight is ideal for casting small flies, but in windy conditions they can be extremely difficult to cast. These lines are designed for fishing flies in sizes 14–28 with tippets of 4–8X. A leader butt of approximately 0.017-diameter monofilament should be used. The leader butt is the large end of the leader that will be attached to the tapered end of the fly line.

No. 5 weight lines are an excellent choice for the angler starting to fish with a fly rod. Although some delicacy is forfeited, the added weight makes it easier to cast a wider range of fly sizes, including small- to medium-size streamers. No. 5 weight is ideal for trout and panfish anglers who don't require an extremely long cast. No. 5 weight line is usually used with dry flies in sizes 12–22 and streamer flies in size 4 and smaller, with tippets of 3–7X and a leader butt of approximately 0.019 diameter of monofilament. Nos. 6 and 7 weight lines are probably the middle of the presentation scale for measuring delicacy and power. They are ideal for casting larger, more wind resistant trout flies, even under windy conditions like those found on larger streams, especially out West. Because of their weight, they are the first choice for the angler who fishes primarily with streamers. For the bass angler, Nos. 6 and 7 weight lines are also available in a bass-bug taper for heavier bass flies. Nos. 6 and 7 weight lines are used with dry flies and nymphs in sizes 8 to the very smallest in sizes 22 and even smaller with a tippet of 0X–5X and a leader butt of 0.021-diameter monofilament.

Nos. 8 and 9 weight lines are up on the power side of the scale. They are most often used by steelhead and salmon fishermen who need the added power to cast large heavy flies. These lines in bass-bug tapers are the preferred choice of bass anglers who cast large wind-resistant bugs. For light-tackle saltwater anglers, these lines are also available in a saltwater taper and are usually used for fishing bass bugs and saltwater flies as well as large dry flies and streamers in sizes 3/0–4, with a tippet of 2X or larger and leader butt of approximately 0.023-diameter monofilament.

Nos. 10–12 weight lines are at the high end of the power scale. Their main purpose is to cast very large wind-resistant flies and poppers with maximum effectiveness. These lines are the first choice of anglers who do a great deal of saltwater fishing, where long cast is often required. Weight-forward saltwater tapers are available for line weights 10–12. Nos. 10–12 weight lines are most often used for fishing salmon and saltwater fish with flies in sizes 4/0–2, with a tippet of 0X or larger and a leader butt of 0.025-diameter monofilament.

Line function refers to what the line does after it hits the water. Some lines float, some sink, and some do both. There are three types of lines:

1. Floating (F). The floating line for most people is the easiest to cast, especially for beginners. Floating lines are used when the fish are either on the surface or near the surface. One of the advantages of the floating line is the visibility of the line, especially during early-morning or evening hours.
2. Sinking (S). Since most species of fish feed below the surface 90 percent of the time, a sinking line is often used. Many of these lines come with various sink rates.
3. Floating/sinking (F/S). The main body of these lines floats, while the front section, the tip, sinks. Color: Bright colors, such as light green or yellow, are easier to see in the air and on the water, which makes the line easier to control.

Line Tapers

Fly lines come with different tapers, which are designed to make casting easier and improve the presentation of the fly. When the line is cast, the energy transferred to the line at the beginning of the cast is carried along the length of the line to the leader, the tippet, and then the fly. To provide less resistance to the transfer of this energy along the line, fly lines are tapered. There are several different configurations for these tapers.

Double taper (DT), as the name suggests, means tapered at each end of the line. Starting at one end, the line gradually increases diameter for the first 20 feet of its length. The line then maintains this diameter for about 50 feet and then gradually reduces the diameter for the last 20 feet. The double taper is a very popular design, since it can be used for most kinds of fishing and enables the line to be cast most delicately. This is also the easiest line to roll-cast (see chapter 6), which is important when trees and other obstructions won't allow a standard backcast. One of the best advantages of this line is that when the working end of the line becomes worn and frayed, the line can be reversed on the spool. The economics are self-evident.

Weight-forward (WF) lines make longer casts easier, especially in windy conditions or on big, fast-flowing water. On these lines the bulk of the weight is at one end of the line, and it is this weight that actually shoots the line out from the rod. The weighted front portion is approximately 30 feet long and is tapered. This line is very popular with floating lines and is probably the most frequently used taper with sinking lines. The WF line is highly recommended to anyone just starting fly-fishing.

Bass-bug tapers (BBT) and saltwater tapers (SWT) are basically weight-forward lines with a shorter, bulkier front taper that helps cast the large, wind-resistant flies that bass and saltwater fishing most often require.

Shooting taper (ST), sometimes called a shooting head, is designed for a very long cast. Basically, it is a tapered 30-foot line (instead of the normal 90 feet), spliced to a special running line of small-diameter fly line or monofilament line. Because of this small-diameter, smooth running line, which is attached to the reel, the shooting taper can be cast for 120 feet or more. This line is difficult to control and is not recommended for anyone just starting fly-fishing.

Level (L) line is uniform in diameter from one end to the other with no taper. It doesn't have much versatility. The neophyte will learn to cast much better with a weight-forward tapered fly line.

LEADERS

Leaders transfer the casting energy from the fly line to the fly, which enables the fly to land on the water in a most natural state. It must disperse the energy so that the fly will land just like an insect on the water. It must also be strong enough to land a large fish but nearly invisible. It must allow the fly to drift freely to give the appearance of a naturally drifting insect. A leader must be tapered to slow down the speed of the cast so that the fly lands gently on the water the way a natural insect would. The tippet, the extreme end of the leader, must be very thin and almost invisible to provide a drag-free float, yet strong enough to hold the fish without breaking off from the line. In general, the fly line has a pound test rating (a measure of line strength in pounds) that far exceeds the strength of the leader.

Since there are different types of leaders, the angler can use the one that will be most convenient for his or her needs and/or special fishing circumstances. Leaders are most often designated by test in pounds, by diameter in thousands, and by an X number, such as 2X, 3X, etc. All leaders are tapered, with the larger-diameter end (called the butt) attaching to the fly line and the smaller-diameter end (called the tippet) attaching to the fly. The size of the butt may vary from as much as 0.028 diameter and 32 pounds, down to as small a tippet as 0.0032 inches in diameter, called 8X, and about a pound in strength. Most leaders come pretapered or knotless from the manufacturer. You can also buy kits and tie your own compound leaders. Manufactured leaders usually come in 7 1/2-, 9-, and 12-foot lengths. The best length for the beginner is the 7 1/2-foot, since they are the easiest to cast and operate and very good for dry-fly, wet-fly, and nymph fishing. Longer leaders are used for smooth, clear waters where the distance between the fly and the fly line is more important than in water with more turbidity.

The most popular leaders are:

1. Knotless tapered leaders. These are very good in weeds or other debris. They are simple to use and are readily available in a variety of lengths and diameters. They can easily be modified by tying on additional lengths of tippet material.
2. Compound leaders. These leaders are made up of different-diameter sections of leader material and are held together with

knots. They will collect weeds and debris more easily than the knotless leaders, but you can tie them together yourself by using different-diameter tippet material.

3. Braided leaders. These are made up of a braided nylon leader section, with a standard tippet section attached for tying the fly to. The braided advantage is that it does not have to be straightened after being stored on the reel. You can also use different tippet sections to match the size of the hook on the fly.

It is important to understand that in dry fly-fishing especially, it is the tippet diameter, or size, that determines the size of the fly you can use. If you cast a heavy No. 10 fly attached to an 8X tippet, the very thin monofilament won't develop enough velocity to carry the fly to the target. It will collapse, causing wind knots and line tangles. A tippet that is too large for a small fly will develop too much speed and slap the water with the fly and spook the fish. Check the following chart to match your tippet to the proper-size fly.

TIPPETS

The tippet is the extreme end of the fly-line system, which can then be attached to the fly for presentation to the fish. The tippet is attached to the end of the leader. Tippet sizes are identified by an X number for diameter of the material. There is no taper to a tippet. One of its advantages is that it is relatively easy to replace at the end of the leader. This becomes more important, since it tends to get shorter and shorter after you replace several flies. Replacement of a tippet is also much more economical than replacement of a leader.

The tippet diameter should be matched to the size of the fly you will use. Too small a tippet will not allow a large fly to turn over properly. Too large a tippet will cause an unnatural drag on a small fly. As a guide to selection of the proper tippet size for the fly you've chosen, there is a formula that can be used. Divide the fly size by 4 and add 1 to the X size for the proper tippet. For example, if you are using a size-16 fly, you would use a 5X tippet. The following chart illustrates the relationship between tippet size and hook size.

Tippet Diameter (inches)	Fly-Hook Size	Pound Test
.011 (0X)	1/0, 2, 4	10
.010 (1X)	2, 4, 6	8.5
.009 (2X)	6, 8, 10	7
.008 (3X)	10, 12, 14	6
.007 (4X)	12, 14, 16	5
.006 (5X)	14, 16, 18	4
.005 (6X)	16, 18, 20, 22	3
.004 (7X)	20, 22, 24, 26	2
.003 (8X)	24, 26, 28	1.2

Tippet length may vary between 18 and 36 inches. Shorten the tippet if using large flies and the leader lands in a tangle on the water. Smaller flies may require longer tippets. Refer to the chart for the proper relationship of tippets to hook sizes.

HOOKS

Probably the most overlooked or ignored piece of tackle by fishermen or fisherwomen is the hook. The wrong hook can defeat even the most expert angler, especially the hooks used for fly-fishing. The different sizes and various kinds of hooks can be mind-boggling. The importance of the hook might be illustrated by reviewing a most common experience when fishing for trout. Very often a trout will merely "suck" in the fly, nymph, or streamer. The instant the fish determines that the fly is a fraud, he will spit the fly out of his mouth. When even the slightest disturbance of the fly line is detected, the hook must be immediately set. A short but fast wrist movement is normally all that is needed, but the hook must be the proper size, and sharp! Too often novice trout anglers assume that a trout will strike a fly in the same manner as a bass or even a bluegill will strike a popper.

Feeding habits of trout are very different from other fish. This is the reason that trout anglers very often use what is called a "strike" indicator attached to the end of the floating fly line or the beginning of the leader when fishing with an underwater fly, such as a nymph or a wet fly. A strike indicator is a piece of bright-colored flannel or putty and should be a part of every trout angler's tackle box. The indicator will dip beneath the surface of the water when a trout sucks in the fly with the initial strike. When the angler sees the indicator dip beneath the water surface, the hook must be set immediately before the fish spits out the artificial fly. Hooks are identified by the dimensions of the various hook parts (see Fig. 6). The hook parts are the eye where the tippet is attached to the hook (fly) and the shank, which determines the length of the hook. In general, short hooks are used for dry flies and nymphs, and longer hooks are used for streamers and bucktails. The bend is that part of the hook that is bent, usually in a short radius that forms the throat of the hook. The point with its barb is that extension of the bend that is now parallel with the shank. The gap is the distance of the point to the shank.

There are many different configurations to these hook parts by the various manufacturers, for example, hollow points, curved points, tapered eye, ball eye, etc. For the novice starting to fly-fish, it should be sufficient to know that it is best to avoid hooks with extremely long shanks, which are used for larger fish. Standard-weight wire hooks are the best, and single hooks will catch more

Figure 6. The basic elements of a hook

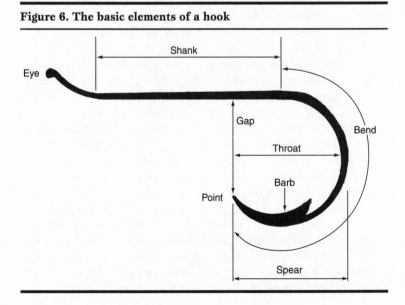

fish than double or triple hooks. For fly-fishing, the best hook sizes are Nos. 8, 10, 12, 14, 16, 18, 20, and 22. The most commonly used hooks are Nos. 10 and 12. Most important, the points must be sharp. A hook sharpener is an excellent addition to the tackle box. Barbless hooks are also available to make it easier to release fish.

THE MATCHED SET

Rod, Reel, Line, Leader, Tippet, and Fly

One area of confusion and mystery about fly-fishing has been the enigma of the "matched set" or the "matched rod and tackle," etc. There is really no mystery about it. The strength and geometry of all of the materials that make up the fly-fishing tackle should all be compatible with each other so that the operation and function of one item will work smoothly with the operation and function of any other piece of equipment. The length and flexibility of the rod material should "match" the line, which should be compatible with the leader, which has a compatible tippet to match the fly that is being cast. Of course, the reel must be able to store the amount of backing as well as the fly line being used for that fishing day.

If any of these items do not match, trouble can be expected when the angler tries to place the fly on or in the water. If a tippet diameter is too small for the fly, a large fly will not turn over properly. Too big a tippet will cause an unnatural drag on a small dry fly. If a large fly is too heavy for a tippet, wind knots and line tangles will result. If the line doesn't match the rod, casting will not only be difficult but also very tiring, and accuracy will be jeopardized.

For the beginner, a recommended ideal matched set for fishing panfish or small trout might include the following: A 3-ounce weight rod, 8 feet 6 inches long for a No. 6 floating line.

To match this rod and line, use a tapered 5X leader with a 4-pound test tippet. To save money, attach a 36-inch tippet to the tippet at the end of the leader. This is important, since every time you change flies, you will lose some tippet material, and the tippets of leaders will quickly be gone with these changes. Attaching your own tippet will extend the life of your leaders indefinitely.

The fly sizes that will work well for this tackle are Nos. 14, 16, or 18.

Such a matched set of tackle could be modified to suit a particular situation, but remember: The more you bend the rules, the more you compromise good fly-fishing technique. It should be emphasized that one rod, reel, line, and leader won't meet the challenges of every fishing situation.

If you're going to fish steelhead or saltwater bonefish, you will need an 8-foot-6-inch or even a 9-foot rod that weighs 5 1/2 ounces, which would send a heavier WF-8-F line up to a 100 feet. Tackle has to change to meet the different conditions. The most important variable is the size of the fish you are attempting to catch. However, to start fly-fishing, extra-light or extra-heavy tackle is not recommended.

Rod Cases, Tackle Boxes, Fly Boxes, and Wallets

The rod case and its stocking for the rod has to be one of the most important pieces of fly-fishing equipment. So much depends on a good case for your rod. There are many choices, but I believe that the rigid aluminum cases are the best. The soft cases, many of which are very expensive, just won't do when it comes to stuffing them in the trunk of a car or storing them in a closet at the end of the season.

The tackle box is the repository of practically all of the fishing supplies and most of the equipment that will be used for this new form of recreation. Tackle boxes come in all sizes. For the neophyte, the smaller box is probably the best bet. These boxes are relatively inexpensive, and a larger box can easily replace the smaller one as more materials and equipment are added. It should not be too small, though; of course, it should be able to store such things as an extra reel spool, extra fly line, extra leaders, fishing knife, and fly boxes and wallets. You don't have to break the bank to buy a tackle box, but make sure it has good hinges, is not too heavy, and has more than one latch, which can be locked, if necessary. It is hard to imagine a more frustrating experience than to have a fishing-tackle box discharge its contents on the floor or on the ground when you try to pick it up and the latch fails.

A good fly box is one of the best additions to your fly-fishing tackle supplies that you can make. These boxes and wallets come in a wide assortment of styles and prices. Some of the least expensive and most utilitarian are the transparent plastic boxes with many interiors compartments designed to hold a wide assortment of flies. Make sure that these compartments are at least an inch deep and that the box itself can fit into your fishing vest. A step up from the plastic boxes are the aluminum boxes with a plastic foam lining for anchoring the flies of choice for the day. Some of the more expensive boxes even have spring-loaded plastic lids to facilitate the storage and removal of the choice flies. Whatever fly storage box or wallet you have, be sure the flies are all dried out after each fishing trip. Another word of caution: Be sure to remove the flies from their storage container when you apply flotation spray just before you start fishing. Some of the propellants in these spray cans can destroy the plastic in the fly boxes.

CHAPTER 4

Knots and Tackle Assembly

The basic fly-fishing equipment—rod, reel, line backing, fly line, leader, tippet, and fly—must be assembled for a working system. All of these items are fastened together by means of knots. Woe to the angler who ignores knots or assumes he will learn about them when fishing on a lake or stream, which is *not* the place to learn how to tie knots. Asking the guide or a friend to help you under these circumstances may also be an invitation to disaster (especially at night). Learn your knots now and spend some time before each fishing trip to review them. Sooner than you might think, tying these knots will be second nature.

Figure 7 shows the fly-line components and some popular knots that connect them for the complete assembly of the fly-fishing rod, reel, line backing, line, leader, tippet, and the fly.

1. The Duncan loop is one of the best knots for attaching the backing line to the reel. Incidentally, always use braided nylon or Dacron line for backing. Never use monofilament for backing.
2. The nail knot or the Duncan loop are the most common knots used for connecting the backing line to the fly line. Be certain that with a weight-forward line, the backing line is attached to the butt end of the fly line. It makes no difference with a double taper or a level line. Once the knot is completed, coat with clear nail polish or some other clear cement and let dry before winding on the reel.
3. The Duncan-loop knot or the loop-to-loop connection are the most popular for the leader-to-fly-line junction.
4. The surgeon's knot is used to fasten the tippet to the leader. This knot should be wet before it is pulled tight.
5. The Duncan loop or the clinch knot are the most common knots used to connect the tippet to the fly.

Figure 7. Fly-line components and the five knots that fasten them together

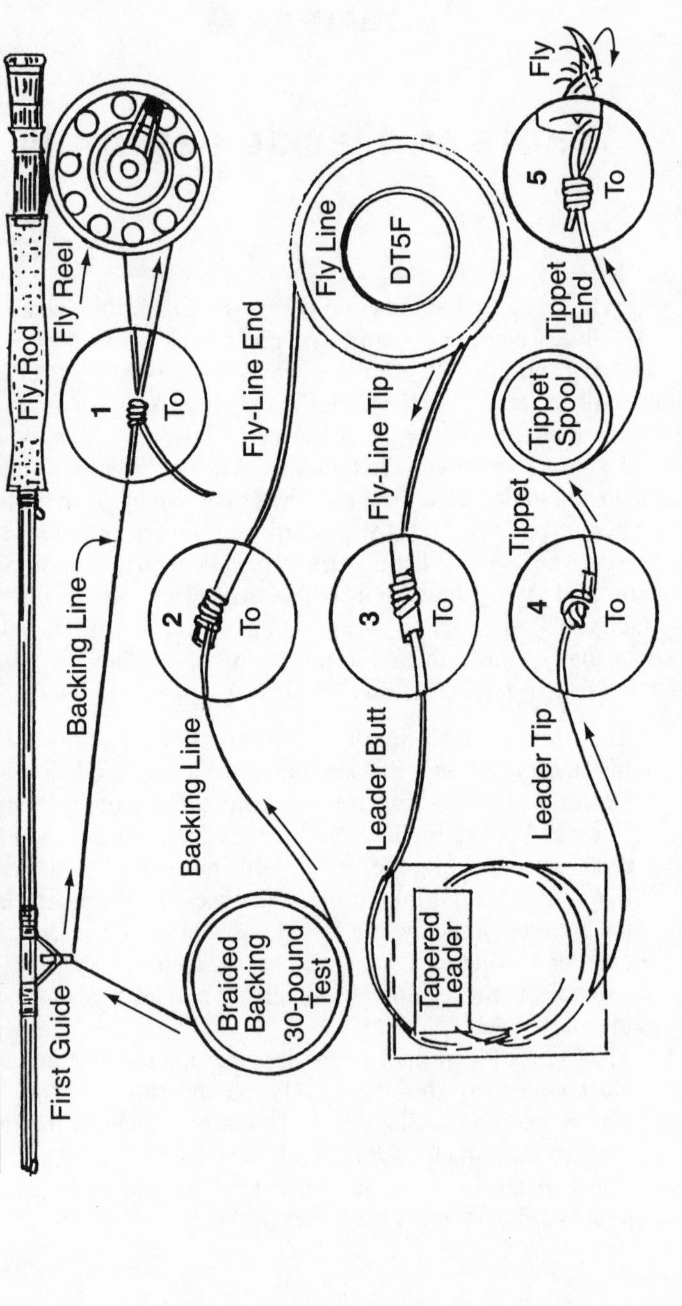

Fly Rod

Fly Reel

Fly Line
DT5F

Fly

1 To

Fly-Line End

Fly-Line Tip

5 To

Tippet End

Tippet Spool

Backing Line

2 To

3 To

4 To

Tippet

Backing Line

Leader Butt

Leader Tip

Braided Backing 30-pound Test

Tapered Leader

First Guide

These five knots and others are described on the following pages (Figs. 8–16). They are the most basic of all knots, and when mastered by the fly-fishing enthusiast, they will satisfy 90 percent of the fishing requirements that will ever be encountered. For the advanced fly-fishing angler, additional tackle and knots will be required, especially for the heavier saltwater fish. Remember also, when learning how to tie these knots, don't start out with monofilament and/or fly line. Instead, begin with two pieces of 1/4-inch chord or rope about 24 or 36 inches long. Don't make an unnecessary amount of work out of the learning process. Take your time and start your exercises at home under relaxed conditions.

Figure 8. Knot No. 1, backing to fly reel, Duncan loop or uniknot

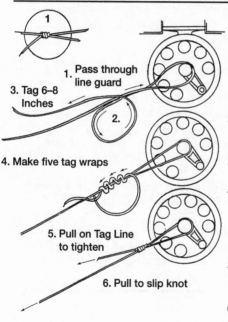

1. Pass through line guard
3. Tag 6–8 Inches
2.
4. Make five tag wraps
5. Pull on Tag Line to tighten
6. Pull to slip knot

1. Pass the backing line through the line guard of the reel and then around the reel spool and back out of the line guard with 8–12 inches of tag end remaining to tie the knot with.
2. Form a large loop with the tag end toward, and then away from the reel.
3. The tag excess should then be about 6–8 inches.
4. With the tag end, make five wraps away from the reel, through the loop, and the standing line as illustrated.
5. Pull on the tag end to tighten the knot over the line.
6. Pull hard on the line to slide and tighten the loop against the spool spindle of the reel. Clip the excess tag end off. Make sure that the knot loop is very tight against the spindle.

Figure 9. Knot No. 2, backing to fly line, Duncan loop

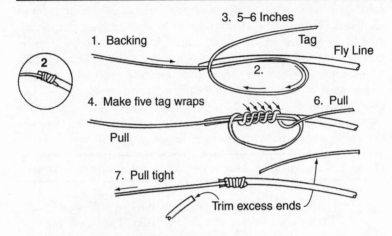

1. Lay 10 inches of backing alongside the end of the fly line.
2. Loop the tag end back toward the fly line end to form a 2-inch loop.
3. The tag end of the backing should be 5 or 6 inches long.
4. With the tag end of the backing, make five wraps over the fly line and through the loop back from the fly-line end.
5. Grasp the fly line and wraps, then carefully pull on the backing to close the slack in the loop. Take care not to allow the knot to slip off the end of the fly line.
6. Pull on the tag end to tighten the knot wraps and loop firmly against the end of the fly line. Try to keep the knot wraps close together but not overlaping.
7. Pull the backing tight and trim the excess fly-line and backing so that you have a neat trouble-free knot. Coat the knot and fly-line end with a flexible waterproof cement to make the connection smoother and stronger.

Figure 10. Knot No. 3, leader to fly line, Duncan loop

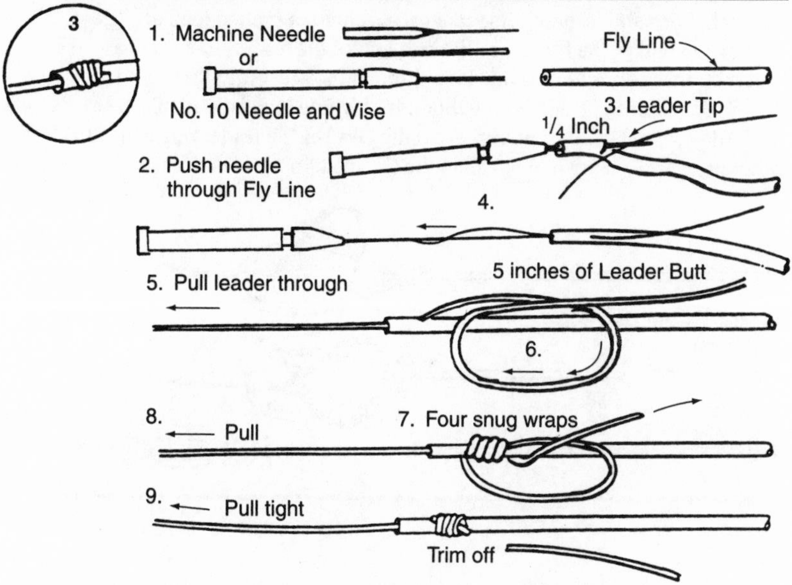

For knotless tapered leaders before the tippet is added.

1. Begin with a size 12 or 10 beading, darning, or small sewing-machine needle.
2. Insert the needle end into the core of the fly line's tip about 1/2 inch; then push it off the side of the coating as illustrated.
3. Pass the leader tip through the eye of the needle. If the tip is too large, shave it with a razor blade until it is small enough to pass through the eye.
4. Pull the needle and end of the leader out of the tip of the fly line.
5. Pull the leader through to about 6 or 8 inches from the end of the butt.
6. With the end of the butt, form a loop next to the fly line, away from the tip end of the line.
7. Holding the fly line and loop firmly, make four snug, close-spaced wraps beginning at the exit hole, around the fly line and through the loop as illustrated. Make sure that you wrap the leader butt away from the fly-line tip end.
8. Take care to keep the leader butt wraps held tightly in place while the leader is pulled to snug up the knot's loop.
9. Make one more extra-hard pull on the leader to snug it well; then trim the excess leader-butt tag end close to the knot. Coat the knot and the tip of the line with a fast-drying cement for a smooth knot.

Figure 11. Leader to fly-line variation

Many fly lines and leaders come in a package with a pretied loop at either the tapered end of the fly line or the butt end of the leader. In either case, the fastest connection is to pass one loop through the other and then through the tippet end of the leader and tighten. If only one loop is available, tie a "tucked sheet bend" knot with the standing end of the leader or fly line. In either case, apply clear nail polish to the finished knot.

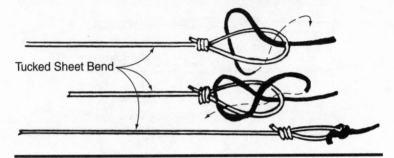

Figure 12. Knot No. 4, tippet to leader, surgeon's knot

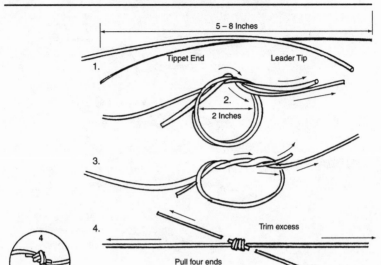

1. Place leader tip and tippet section ends side by side in opposite directions, overlapping 5–7 inches.
2. With the ends together, form a 2-inch-diameter loop and pass the leader tip tag and the tippet's long end through the loop.
3. Pass both through the loop once more. Then wet the loop wraps with saliva or water.
4. Tighten knot by first pulling on the long sides of leader and tippet, then on the tag ends. Trim the excess tag ends.

Figure 13. Fly-to-leader attachment—the Duncan loop

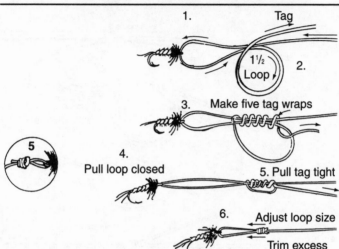

Knot No. 5, tippet or tip to fly, Duncan loop.

1. Pass 6–8 inches of tag end of tippet through the eye of the hook.
2. First toward, then away from the fly, form a 1 1/2-inch-diameter loop with the tag.
3. Pass the tag through and around the loop and tippet five times. Make sure that the wraps are away from the fly.
4. Wet the wraps with saliva and snug five wraps by holding on to the tag and pulling the fly as illustrated.
5. Tighten knot by pulling very tightly on the tag end. The degree of the tightening determines how the knot will slide on the tippet for keeping the loop open or slipping it closed. If using a heavy tippet, over 0.011 inch, tighten the knot with pliers.
6. Adjust the loop between the fly hook and the knot to the desired size for a specific fly performance. Trim the excess tag.

Figure 14. Clinch knot

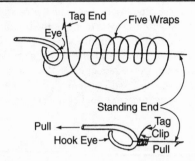

One of the most versatile and easiest knots for tying the fly to the tippet is the clinch knot. With a little practice it can even be tied in the dark.

1. After passing the tippet through the eye of the hook, make five wraps around the tippet standing end and then pass the tag end back through the first loop at the eye of the hook.
2. Wet the assembled knot with water or saliva.
3. Pull on the hook eye and the standing end of the tippet to tighten the knot. Do not pull on the tag end of the tippet to tighten.
4. Clip off the tag end at the eye of the hook.

Improved clinch knot

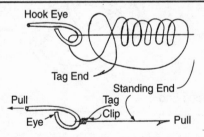

5. For the improved clinch knot, pass the tag end back through the loop from the wraps around the standing end of the tippet.
6. Then tighten by pulling on the eye of the hook and the standing end of the line.

Figure 15. Surgeon's loop

This is one of the most versital knots for the angler or anyone. It is only an overhand knot made with the looped end of the line. A second wrap with the loop makes it a surgeon's knot.

By putting a surgeon's loop on the end of a leader, a fast loop-to-loop connection can be used to change leaders quickly. Put a second loop in the butt end of the new leader and pass one loop through the other to make the connection. The same procedure applies for loop-to-loop leader to tippet changes.

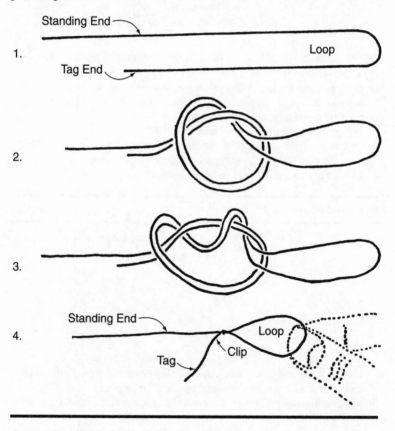

Figure 16. Double surgeon's knot

The double surgeon's knot is used to tie the tippet to the leader. It works very well for joining two different-diameter monofilament lines in tippet sections of the leader. You should wet this knot before you pull it tight. Wind the leader on the reel except for the last 8 or 10 inches of the end. Pass this end through one of the holes in the side of the reel. This prevents the end from getting buried under the line coils and makes it easy to assemble your tackle for the next fly-fishing.

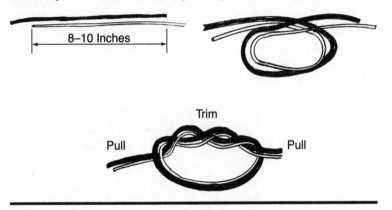

ASSEMBLING THE ROD AND TACKLE

With all of the backing, fly line, leader, and tippet on the reel, the next step is to mount the reel onto the fly rod. First, remove the fly rod from its sturdy tube case and its cloth stocking. Next, you must decide which side of the reel you want the reel handle. If you are right-handed and will cast with your right hand, you may want the reel handle on the left-hand side of the rod so you can reel the line onto the reel with your left hand. Or you may prefer to switch the rod to your left hand after the cast and reel the line in with your right hand. This is a matter of personal choice, so set the spool on the reel where you think you would like it. You can always change later. In any event, make sure that the line guard of the reel is facing forward. Now tighten the reel-seat lock so that the reel fits snug in the reel seat. Do not use pliers to tighten the reel-seat lock. Finger-tight only!

It's now time to string the rod up with the fly line, leader, and tippet for real fishing with the fly rod. There are many ways to do this. One of the most simple methods is to double the fly line over on itself and thread this loop through the rod guides instead of using the tippet to start this task. This method is easy. If the fly line slips from your fingers, it will not slide back through the guides and frustrate you. You may now add the leader, a tippet, and finally an artificial fly to the fly for a complete assembly. Once the fly is attached to the tippet, place the spear of the hook onto the hook keeper just above the fly rod handle. Of course, you could add these to the fly line before the line is strung through the rod, but for the first assembly, it may be easier to string the rod first. After the tackle is all assembled, when you pick up the rod to move to the practice field to start fly-casting, be sure to walk with the rod handle and reel pointed forward and the tip section of the rod pointed behind you. This is the safest procedure and avoids trees, bushes, etc. Now that your rod and tackle are ready to go, you're ready to learn how to fly-cast and/or start fishing with your fly rod.

CHAPTER 5

Fly-Fishing Accessories

Since fly-fishing is an outdoor sport and most often occurs some distance away from the comfort and convenience of urban living, it is important and most desirable to have good clothing and some essential accessories to complement your fishing outing. In most cases, the fishing trip is a vacation, and nobody wants to be miserable or disappointed on a vacation. The following list of clothing and equipment is directed at the actual fishing situation as distinct from normal travel gear and accessories. This list might also be used as a punch list to check off just before departure to your favorite lake or stream.

CLOTHING AND APPAREL

1. Underwear is one of the most important requirements for spending any time either on or in the water of a cold-water trout stream. Trout streams normally have temperatures of 50–60 degrees Fahrenheit. Boots, waders, or trousers won't be sufficient for your legs even if the air temperatures are in the seventies. A good set of long underwear in addition to your more personal underclothing is the answer. It can be made from wool, cotton, polypropylene, or some combination of these materials. These are the same materials that skiers wear for their underclothes where temperatures often fall below freezing. Doing so will avoid leg cramps and pain and discomfort during the night.

2. A water-repellent fishing hat with a wide brim and a chin strap is considered essential by many anglers. Whatever hat you choose, make sure it has a beak to shade your eyes from the

sun. The hat not only protects your head from the sun and an occasional branch or even a misplaced fly; it will also keep you warm. The chin strap will keep the hat with you during a sudden wind gust. It's not easy to chase a hat floating down a stream. In addition, remember you are never completely dressed unless you wear a hat.

3. A fishing vest is an absolute must for fly-fishing. There are countless varieties of these vests, so it will come down to personal choice, but be sure there are enough pockets to carry and organize all of the numerous items you might use for each venture into the water. The vest will be your personal valet. If there is any concern about the waters you are going to wade in for your fishing or boating or you just plain can't swim, you should consider an inflatable supervest. This provides an excellent and comfortable margin of safety when wading or boating in deep or fast water. It is a bit more expensive, but the reassurance and comfort are well worth it.

4. Warm stockings of wool, cotton, or some of the more modern materials used for skiing, hiking, or hunting. Cold feet can spoil any fishing trip. Trout streams are especially cold.

5. Warm shirts with long sleeves and high collars should be in the clothing ensemble. Avoid short sleeves and lightweight blouses or T-shirts. The sun's rays reflecting off the water along with the occasional encounter with mosquitoes and/or black flies can inflict severe punishment on exposed skin.

6. Sweaters that can be added or removed as needed for comfort. Even in midsummer the temperature can drop 20 degrees by nightfall.

7. Outdoor trousers with additional side leg pockets are most convenient.

8. Rain and wind jackets that fold up into very compact packages are a welcome addition to cope with a sudden rainstorm. A hood with a drawstring is a good addition. Avoid plastic that cracks or gets stiff in cold weather.

9. Gloves may be desirable if you intend to fish at high altitudes or late in the season in cold weather. Be sure they are suitable for handling your fly rod and tackle. Fingerless fleece or wool gloves allow you to fish in comfort in cool weather, but for very cold late fall, winter, and early spring fishing, neoprene gloves

are the best. These gloves are about 1 millimeter thick, which permits maximum dexterity under the circumstances.

10. One old pair of tennis shoes or lightweight athletic shoes that are ready to be discarded are highly recommended. Trekking along the water's edge of a lake or stream to explore the current aquatic insect hatches as well as the best points to enter the stream for wading is very often required for the proper reconnaissance before you put on your boots or waders. If your fishing trip will include any boating on the lake or river, a good pair of boat shoes or tennis shoes are a must to permit easy on or easy off and avoid slipping on the boat deck or the dock.

ACCESSORIES AND EQUIPMENT FOR FLY-FISHING

1. Wading boots
2. Small shoulder bag or knapsack for important equipment, for example, extra reels, extra spools, wading-boots patch kits, fish knife, fishing books, maps of stream or lake, etc.
3. Sharp scissors
4. Needle-nose pliers. Be sure these pliers have wire-cutting blades at the base of the pinchers.
5. Nail clippers
6. Different tippet spools with labels
7. Polarized sunglasses. One of the most important assets for the angler. These glasses not only protect the eyes, but they cut the glare from the water and allow you to see the fly, underwater objects, and the fish in the water much better. An elastic band to hold the glasses around your neck is important so that they don't drop into the water.
8. Dry fly spray
9. Strike-indicator putty or flannel
10. Insect-repellent spray or bottle
11. Fly boxes and/or wallets
12. Thermometer (submersible) for reading stream or lake temperatures.
13. Landing net
14. Creel

15. Waterproof wallet for car keys, money, and fishing license
16. Wading staff
17. Head net for insect protection to be stored on or in fishing hat
18. Matches in waterproof container
19. Good pocketknife with scissors, screwdriver blade, punch, and cork screw
20. Small flashlight. Don't forget the batteries.
21. Sun block
22. Compass
23. Band-Aids
24. Patch kit for boots
25. Small plastic bottle for drinking water
26. Aspirin or Tylenol
27. Zinger (retractable cord), especially for the landing net as well as any other frequently used piece of equipment
28. Handkerchief and/or Kleenex packets
29. Surgical forceps are one of the best tools known for removing a fly from a fish's mouth.
30. Fishing tackle box for carrying extra fly line, split-shot lead sinkers, leaders, flies, reel spools, hooks, fishing literature, tippets, clippers, knife, etc.

Everything on this list (except the knapsack, creel, boots, tackle box, landing net, and staff) should either fit into the pockets of your clothing or into the pockets of your fishing vest so that it can be accessible while fishing.

Under some circumstances, such as a long day trip in a river-boat, you may want to carry this additional equipment:

1. Waterproof watch
2. Camera enclosed in a waterproof case
3. Binoculars
4. Some candy bars or health-food bars
5. Thermos bottle with hot soup or coffee
6. A picnic lunch or materials for a shore lunch
7. Extra sweater and/or warm jacket
8. Extra pair of warm stockings
9. Small towel and/or Kleenex packs
10. Waterproof shoulder bag that will float to carry all of these items

11. First-aid kit
12. Additional water bottle or canteen
13. Paper plates, plastic knives, spoons, and forks
14. Plastic tablecloth or ground-cover fabric
15. Fly-rod case
16. Extra reel and fly line

The most important piece of equipment an angler uses, along with the rod and reel, are the waders (boots) needed to enter the stream or even the lake shoreline. Hip boots are fine for wading small streams or any waters that are not too deep, but full-chest waders are needed for most of the fishing conditions the angler will encounter. There are two types of full-chest waders, the boot-foot wader and the stocking-foot wader. Both types are very good, but neither one is perfect for every situation. Generally, if one has to walk some distance before entering the water, the stocking-foot wader has some advantage. The stocking-foot wader, which is a full-chest wader, does require a separate wading shoe to be placed over the foot part of the wader. The boot-foot wader, with the boot attached to the lower part of the wader, is a single unit and has the advantage of being more convenient to put on or off.

No matter which type of waders you choose, it is important that the bottom of the shoes or boots have soles to prevent slippage on the wet rocks or hard rubber cleats to grip the sandy bottoms of many lakes and streams. If most of your wading will be in streams with bottoms of sand or gravel, rubber-soled shoes with hard rubber cleats will be most satisfactory. But where the bottom is rocky and/or made up or large, round rocks and boulders, felt soles are essential. Although some boot-foot waders are made with felt soles and do a good job, the felt soles wear out long before the boots do, and are not easy to replace. Felt-soled sandals are available and not too expensive. These can fit over the rubber-soled boots and have the advantage of making one pair of waders available for both stream conditions. By removing the sandals when they are not needed, the felt bottoms can last indefinitely. Metal cleats are also available for special conditions. When purchasing waders, it is most important to wear heavy wool socks for a proper fit of the boot to the foot. Warm socks are essential for avoiding cold feet when wading.

The primary function of the waders is to keep you dry and protect you from the bone-chilling cold of many rivers and lakes. Waders are made of either rubber, neoprene, or nylon and do an excellent job as long as they are not abused. They will rip and tear on a barbed-wire fence or a car-door slam, but most of the time they can be easily patched. Always carry a patch repair kit on your fishing trips. When using these boots, make sure that the safety belt is drawn up tight and worn at all times while in the water so that an accidental spill won't result in the waders filling with water.

A raincoat is essential for any fly-fisher. For boat fishing it should be long and full-skirted. For wading in the stream or lake, it should be short and of course very light. Today these requirements are easy to satisfy. Modern rain gear made of nylon and other materials is available in almost any style one can imagine. It is almost weightless and can be rolled up into small balls that will fit into your hand or stuff into your tackle box. Some of it even comes rolled up into a fanny pack with no sacks to lose. The fabric of this rain gear is treated with waterproof polyurethane, and the seams are treated with heat tape. Most of these raincoats are two-piece suits, so the lower rain pants can be left off if waders are used when in the stream. All of this gear is readily available for women as well as men today.

CHAPTER 6

Fly-Casting

Fly-casting is an important part of fly-fishing, but it is not the most important part. Too many anglers starting to fish with a fly rod are intimidated by the stories and movies of the "master" anglers who cast 90 or 100 feet in a lake or stream. Forget it. In any event, don't be intimidated. Most fish taken on a fly are hooked within 10–20 feet from the angler. What is important by far is the accuracy and control of the fly cast. Also remember that it is essential to practice this art form in order to achieve even a reasonable degree of proficiency. It's like learning to swim. All of the books, movies, and lectures in the world will not make you a good swimmer until you get into the water and practice. Remember, casting while fishing is not practice. Use the lawn or a swimming pool. It is very helpful for you, the beginner, to learn and understand the basic principles of good casting technique early on so that when you start casting, you won't develop bad habits with improper techniques. Of course, a good instructor is an excellent help to get started, but in the absence of an experienced teacher, good manuals and videotapes, along with a friendly coach, can help you with your practice. In the absence of a coach, try to work with another student who can watch your technique and point out your errors and/or improper techniques. Since you can't watch yourself, an observant coach can be a big help when you're starting out. There are really only two basic casts to learn. They are the overhead cast and the roll cast. All other casts are variations and different movements of these two.

CASTING PRINCIPLES

The purpose of casting the fly is to deliver the fly to the target as effectively as possible. It is the flexing (loading) and relaxing (unloading) of the rod that makes the line work to deliver the fly. Great strength is not required. In fact, too much strength with a cast most often results in loss of control and a bad cast. It is the weight of the line and the velocity of the cast that loads (flexes) the rod and imparts kinetic energy into the rod and the line.

It is the arm movement with the twist of the wrist that sets the rod in motion (unloading) so that the line can be delivered. Stand so that you are at 45 degrees from a line with the target. In this way, you can watch the backcast and still present the forward cast from your standing position. To grip the rod properly, hold the rod firmly with your casting hand and place your thumb on top of the rod grip. The baseball grip is also good, but don't grip the rod with the forefinger on top of the rod handle. This is the easiest way to lose control of the rod.

THE OVERHEAD CAST

The basic overhead cast is made up of a backcast and a forward cast (Figs. 17 and 18). The best way to describe these motions is to compare the positions of the fly rod to the hands of a clock. With the rod held straight up in a vertical position, it matches the 12 o'clock position on the clock. With the rod laid back over the shoulder parallel to the ground, the rod would be in the 9 o'clock position on the clock, and with the rod extended straight out, forward and parallel to the ground, it would be in the 3 o'clock position of the clock. It's important for the novice to understand these positions in these terms, since most all references to fly-casting are expressed in terms of the hands-of-the-clock positions.

THE BACKCAST

The first step for the backcast is to strip off from the reel about 20 feet of fly line. Now swing the rod from left to right in a horizontal plane to move all of the line you've stripped from the reel through all of the rod guides so that the line is now lying on the water (or lawn) in front of you. Then hold the fly line in your left hand (if you are casting with your right hand) about level with your waist.

Next, point the tip of the rod at the target, holding the rod in the 3 o'clock position. You should now have about 15 or 20 feet of line hanging out from the rod tip on the water. Then raise the rod to about the 2 o'clock position. The weight of the line will cause the rod to flex (load) somewhat. Now rapidly move the rod to the 12 o'clock position and stop the stroke at that point while the line continues to extend itself behind you. Slowly, allow your arm to reach the 11 o'clock position and stop right there! The line should now extend to its full length behind you. This extension is also called the "extended reach back." The most common mistake made by anglers starting to cast with a fly rod is made right here by allowing the rod to continue past the 11 o'clock position. Anathema to fly-casting it will defeat the entire operation. This is an important part of control, and for some people it is difficult to master. It can be a big help if the casting arm is held close to the body during the cast. Holding a book or a flat bottle under the arm is helpful. Don't drink the contents of the bottle! At the end of the backcast, the line should be fully extended behind you and parallel to the water. It is most important that the line is allowed to completely straighten out behind you on the backcast; otherwise, it will not go forward on the forward cast in a straight line toward the target. In addition, the line may well act like a whip if brought forward before it has been fully extended on the backcast. The whip can easily snap off the fly or even the entire tippet. Remember that the crack of a whip is actually the breaking of the sound barrier. Don't risk breaking the sound barrier. Make sure that the line is fully extended on the backcast. You are now ready to start the forward cast.

THE FORWARD CAST

The first forward casting movement is the "punch." Once the line has been fully extended on the backcast, the casting arm should be "punched" straightforward with the rod still in the 11 o'clock position. With the casting arm fully extended, the wrist should now snap the rod forward toward the target, but stopping at the 2 o'clock position. With this movement, the line begins to move forward toward the target. As the line begins this forward movement, a loop in the line is formed that unfurls as the line continues toward the target. With good line control and accuracy, the loop of the fly line will be tight and even. A quick flick of the wrist will produce a tight loop. A slow flick of the wrist creates a wide loop. When the line becomes fully extended from the forward cast, it will fall to the surface of the water, with the fly on the tippet landing right where the tip of the rod is pointing.

SHOOTING THE LINE

The initial overhead cast is usually made with about 15 or 20 feet of line laid out on the water, ready for the pickup for the backcast and then the forward cast to the target. After one or two of these casts, it is most often desired to cast the line farther out than the first cast of 20 feet or so. To accomplish this goal, first strip off the reel about 5 or even 10 feet of line. This line will now be floating on the water or coiled in the left hand. This line is now held with the left hand between thumb and forefinger, just in front of the stripper guide, to feed the line out at the completion of the forward cast. The line is not released by the left hand until the forward cast is fully extended out toward the target. The forward momentum of the line will pull the additional line through the stripper guide toward the target. This is the "shootout."

With a smooth backcast and an accurate forward cast for a good shootout of additional line with the casting hand, the left hand can again be brought into play to strip more line from the reel, to hold tension on the line during the pickup, and to backcast and start a longer forward cast. With a little practice, the shooting line can thus add 10–20 feet to the cast. Once the cast is complete, the left hand is used to retrieve the fly and the line back through the stripping guide and coiled into the left hand, ready for the next shoot or forward cast.

THE ROLL CAST

The roll cast (Fig. 19) is one of the most useful and practical casts for any kind of fishing. It is most often used when there is a large obstruction behind the angler, which prevents a backcast for the normal overhead cast. The roll cast is easy to execute, but it must be

Figure 17. The backcast

THE REACH FORWARD
Strip the line off the reel and lay
the line on the water. Hold the
rod at 2 o'clock.

THE LIFT
Raise the rod from 2 o'clock
to 12 o'clock.

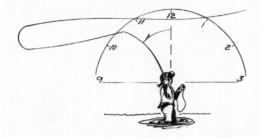

THE BACKCAST
A rapid thrust back from 12 o'clock
to 11 o'clock.

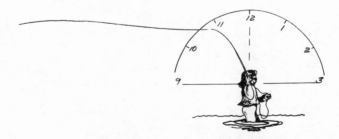

THE EXTENDED REACH BACK
Hold the rod at 11 o'clock until the line
is completely extended back. Most important.

Figure 18. The forward cast

FAST FORWARD
Thrust the rod arm straight out from the
11 o'clock position like a boxer's right
jab to the jaw of his opponent.

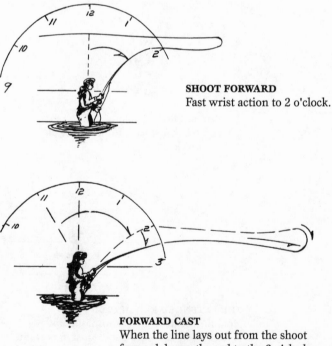

SHOOT FORWARD
Fast wrist action to 2 o'clock.

FORWARD CAST
When the line lays out from the shoot
forward, lower the rod to the 3 o'clock
position and point the rod tip at the target.

Figure 19. The roll cast

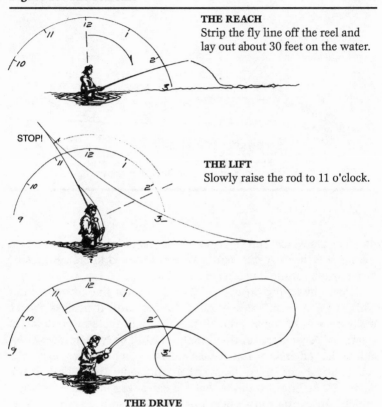

THE REACH
Strip the fly line off the reel and
lay out about 30 feet on the water.

THE LIFT
Slowly raise the rod to 11 o'clock.

THE DRIVE
Fast-forward the rod from 11 o'clock to 2 o'clock.
As the rod is driven forward, the line will roll out.

(Figure 19 continued)

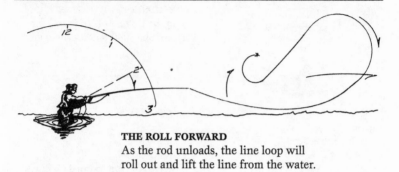

THE ROLL FORWARD
As the rod unloads, the line loop will
roll out and lift the line from the water.

done on the water. You can't do a good job of learning this cast on
the lawn or in the gymnasium. Water is needed to create the surface tension for the line to operate effectively.

Begin by laying off about 20 or 30 feet of line on the water.
This is the "reach." Slowly raise the rod until it reaches the 11
o'clock position. This is the "lift." Stop right there or you'll be in
the trees. A good part of the line should still be lying in the water.
When the rod and the line have come to a complete stop, drive the
rod forward and flick the wrist at the same time. This is the
"drive." The line still in the water creates tension and resistance,
which causes the rod to flex and load. As the rod is driven forward, it begins to unload, and the line begins to roll out. This is
the "roll." As the line rolls up and out, it will deliver the fly to its
target.

MENDING THE LINE

Very often when you are fishing across the current of a stream, the
current will push a major part of the line between the leader and
the tip of the rod into a curve or belly pointed downstream. The
thicker part of the line behind the front-end taper catches more of

the current, and this part of the line moves downstream faster than the tip or the fly. This belly in the line on the water pulls at the floating fly and causes it to move downstream much faster than the natural flow of the current. With a dry fly this is called "drag" and will spook the ever-wary fish. With a wet fly or streamer, this accelerated movement moves the fly faster than any natural food might swim. No fish will take these fast-moving flies. You have to slow these flies down. Mending the line will slow down the flies to the natural state.

Use an upstream mend to take the belly out of the line and slow the drift or the swing of the fly. To mend the line, point the rod tip down the line, then swiftly lift the rod outward and upward and roll it upstream. The line will lift with the rod, arc over, and land on the water again in an "upstream" belly. Often it is necessary to repeat the mend several times on a single cast to continue the proper or natural drift of the fly. Sometimes when fishing very slow water, it may be desirable to mend the line with a downstream mend to speed up the movement of the fly.

THE LINE HAND—HOLDING LOOSE LINE

The line hand is used to gather and hold loops of retrieved line after the cast. This is important when planning a long cast. Each loop held in the hand should hold about 5–10 feet of line. If you hold more than one loop, try to make each successive loop a bit shorter than the one before it so that they won't tangle when you shoot the line.

CHANGING DIRECTIONS OF THE CAST

Very often you will want to lift your line up off the water to cast again in another direction. The line always follows the direction the rod tip follows. Just pick up the line as you normally would and then point the rod toward the new direction on each subsequent backcast and forward cast until you have the line casting where you want it to land. Remember, the fly will land where the rod tip is pointed at the completion of the forward cast.

FLY-CASTING PROBLEMS

Casting problems can arise anytime to frustrate even the most experienced anglers. Here are some of the most common ones:

1. Backcasting down into the water behind you. This is caused by applying too much power through a wide arc (usually past 11 o'clock) for too long a time on the backcast. The remedy is to keep the wrist stiff on the backcast and stop when the rod reaches 11 o'clock. Even try stopping at the 11:30 position until you get it right.

2. So called "wind knots" in the leader and sometimes in the line are caused by pushing the rod too fast through its arc on the backcast and then the forward cast. This can also cause the fly to hook back into the line or the rod. The remedy is to move the rod more slowly through its long arc. Take your time and be smooth with your casting.

3. Snapping the fly and sometimes the leader right off the fly line. This is the "whip" action that is the result of breaking the sound barrier. This problem is caused by starting the forward cast before the backcast has had time to straighten out the line. It is usually the result of a weak backcast with a wide-open loop in the line. The remedy is to make sure that the backcast straightens out the line before the forward cast is started. If you're standing at 45 degrees to your target, watch over your shoulder and keep the loop tight on the backcast.

4. Slapping the water with the line and leader on the forward cast. The main reason for this problem is pointing the tip of the rod too low on the forward cast. The remedy is to stop the forward cast with the rod tip at a higher elevation, say about 2 o'clock, and let the line and leader straighten out 3 or 4 feet above the water so it can land gently without spooking the fish.

5. The line won't straighten and play out on the forward cast. There are two main causes for this problem. First, pushing the rod through a very wide arc on the backcast, say from 3 o'clock to 9 o'clock, with a very wide loop. Second, allowing the line to

slip from your left hand and through the guides of the rod during the backcast and even on the forward cast if you are not shooting the line for a longer cast. The remedy is to make sure that the rod is moving through a small arc, from 2 o'clock to 11 o'clock, with a narrow loop and the line does not play out of your hand until the forward cast is complete.

6. Line and leader tangle at the end of the forward cast. This problem is caused by pushing the rod through a wide arc with a very wide loop. The unbalanced forces on the line in a wide loop are too weak to straighten out the line for its full length, and the forward cast may then force the lower leg of the loop into the upper leg and create a tangle of line and leader. This is one of the most common problems with the neophyte just starting fly-fishing. The remedy is to make sure that the line is fully extended on the backcast from a tight loop and then brought forward with a brisk action from the 11 o'clock position to the 2 o'clock position. Then the rod should be abruptly stopped, allowing kinetic energy of the rod to be transferred into the line for a smooth forward cast in a tight loop and a straight line.

SUMMARY OF FLY-CASTING TECHNIQUES

1. The grip is with a firm grasp, with the thumb on top of the rod handle.
2. The stance is 45 degrees from the direction of the target to allow watching the backcast.
3. The backcast for the overhead cast is made with the arm and wrist action moving the rod from the 2 o'clock position to the 11 o'clock position.
4. The forward cast for the overhead cast is a power stroke with the rod accelerating forward very smoothly through the entire stroke. Then stop abruptly at the 2 o'clock position to form a loop.
5. The fly will land on the water where the rod tip is pointing.
6. For the roll cast, lay out 15–20 feet of line on the water in front of you.

7. Slowly raise the rod until the tip of the rod is at the 11 o'clock position and stop.

8. Rapidly accelerate the rod forward, the "drive," to the 2 o'clock position and stop abruptly. The line should roll across the water in a circular loop about 5 feet high and deliver the fly to the target with a straight leader. If you bring the rod down too far, say to the 3 o'clock position, the line will not form a circular loop.

CHAPTER 7

Fly-Fishing Strategies, Reconnaissance, and Tactics

In any body of water, there is a much greater volume of water than there is of fish. A good reconnaissance combined with a good strategy and good tactics will enhance your fishing success and avoid fishing empty waters. Once it is determined what kind of fish you are fishing for, it's important to survey the water (and even the watershed) to develop some idea about where and how to fish the waters so that the fly can be presented in the most effective manner possible.

RECONNAISSANCE

Where can you go fishing? If you want to start fly-fishing, you must first find someplace to begin fishing. If you have friends who are anglers, especially those who fish with a fly rod, you may get good references from them. Another good source of information is the Internet, which is available on most computers purchased in this country. Generally, any Internet provider will respond to your request on "Fishing" with a map of the United States, asking what region you are interested in. This will be followed by a menu for your selection of what state you are interested in. This, in turn, is followed by a selection of what part of the state you are interested in and then a choice of any one of several publications that are available for your review describing the fishing conditions, for example, weather reports, water temperatures, flow rates, water clarity, hatches, etc., for various parts of the rivers or lakes that are available. Print out a hard copy of this information and you have a head start on your fishing trip. In spite of the fees for this service, it is without a doubt one of the best information services available throughout the country. If your provider doesn't have this service available, check with your local library. Most of them have it.

Otherwise, and in particular, if you are in a strange part of the country, a good place to begin your exploration is the first available fly shop. Not just any dealer, but one who has a wide display of fly-fishing tackle, flies, and good literature. Such a sporting-goods store should have a list of places to fish in the local area as well as out of state. One of the best sources of this information is the State Department of Natural Resources, Fisheries Division, or the State Conservation Department. In either case you will find these people more than willing to help you. Most of the time their whole life is directed at fishing, and they welcome beginners to this most enjoyable and relaxing sport. Don't pass up your local library for this information, especially the magazine and periodical section, which can be a wealth of information on recreation and places to fish and/or guide services.

If possible, use a map for your reconnaissance. You can start this exercise even before you see the water. The better the map, the more information displayed. Look for dimensions, for example, width of stream, depth of water, rapids or fast water, docks and piling, marshes and swamps, tributary streams, rocky or sandy shorelines, etc. With the map and your guide or companion (if you're a novice, don't fish alone!), get some idea where you're going to fish and how long you will be on or in the water. At the same time, you can make an estimate of what time you are going to start fishing. It will make a difference if you are going to fish in the morning, afternoon, or evening. If you're planning this strategy at home; it's also a good idea to get a fix on the date and time of year you will be fishing. If possible, also get a weather report for the area. Is there still snow on the ground (how much?), is it cold or hot, is the water high or low, is there a drought, etc.? Along with the maps and reports, conversations with anyone who has fished the water most recently will provide valuable information for making the right preparations for fishing.

It's especially important to determine what food is available for the fish you are trying to catch. Is there a hatch? If so, what kind? With a hatch, you'll be fishing dry flies. With no hatch, you will be fishing below the water surface with wet flies, nymphs, or streamers.

It's helpful to check the local hatch schedule at this time for the area you will be fishing. When you arrive at the water you will be fishing, observe its surface for a hatch. An investigation along the water's edge can also be very revealing. Look for aquatic insect nymphs on the rocks in the water along the shoreline.

Observe the water surface to locate the areas of fast water, slow water, wave action, eddies, tree overhangs, and quiet pools. Fish are on a continuous quest for food and always practice conservation of energy while struggling for the available food supply. In a river or stream the fish waits for the current to bring his food to him. In a lake or pond the fish may hide behind the leaves of the aquatic vegetation to ambush a smaller fish or insect; in any case, the fish will always try to conserve energy. In a stream the fish will face upstream, waiting for his food. There is always a considerable variation in the velocity of water in a stream because of the frictional drag from the bottom of the stream and the resistance from obstructions, such as rocks, logs, and the changes in direction (bends) in the stream. The fish will therefore avoid the fast water in the middle of the stream and favor the quieter water behind the rocks and logs, near the water's edge, for the best holding position when he is frightened or just resting. The fish's camouflage will offer some protection from airborne predators, but deep water, overhanging bushes, trees, and logs offer the best protection. The predators that the fish have to be concerned about are eagles, owls, osprey, loons, cormorants, and kingfishers that attack from the air. Other predators besides man include bears and raccoons. When looking for places in the water where the fish will hold and/or hide, look for structures in the water, such as logs at, as well as below, the surface of the water, rocks and boulders, overhangs, and trees and bushes at the water's edge. These are the places where you will present your fly to land a fish.

Reconnaissance should tell you whether the bottom of the stream or lake is sand, gravel, marl, or muck. You should also get some idea of how deep the water is, especially in the areas where you will fish, paddle your boat, and/or wade. As noted before, the temperature of the water is very important. When taking the temperature of the water, make more than one measurement at different locations and, if possible, take the temperatures at different times of the day.

If you are going to be in a boat while fishing the lake or the river, be sure to check the weather report. You should never be on or in the water during a thunderstorm. If you are going to be in a boat with a guide, make sure that the vessel is approved for passenger service and carries a full complement of safety devices, including personal floatation devices. If you have a guide, make sure that he understands that you have not fished these waters before and you haven't a clue about what his procedures are. The guide should make it clear to you what the full scope of his or her services are as well as the fees for the fishing trip. Many guides will not offer any coaching or help you with changing flies, assembling your tackle, etc. These guides will limit their services to finding the fishing holes and operating the boat.

Make notes and keep a record of your reconnaissance not only for your own determination of where you are going to fish now but as a reference for your fishing trip next month or next year. Also note the references you received from other anglers when you asked them about their recent fishing experiences. Remember that the main purpose of reconnaissance is to avoid fishing in empty water as much as possible. You want your whole presentation to be where the fish are holding. Note in your records where you caught your fish and the fly you caught him on. These records are also fun to review later in your newfound hobby of fly-fishing.

READING THE WATER

In 90 percent of the water that you see, there are no fish! Fish live somewhere in the remaining 10 percent of the water. They carefully select where they are going to be (hold) in the water to satisfy all of their requirements for survival. Their first requirement is security. Predators from out of the water and in it are a constant threat to the life of a fish. Food supply is essential to the fish, and the conservation of energy is critical if the fish is to continue to feed and be secure. There are three types of water where fly-fishing is most commonly practiced: streams and rivers, which are common throughout America; lakes and ponds, which are also common almost everywhere; and estuaries and tidal flats, which are prevalent along both the Atlantic and Pacific Coasts. Reading each type of water calls for a slightly different technique for each situation.

Streams and rivers are moving bodies of water following a steep or a flat gradient (downhill slope) as it flows toward the sea. This continuous velocity (motion) of water, sometimes fast, sometimes slow, picks up nutrients and minerals from the soil and the streambed, which results in an alkalinity (measured from 1 to 14) that is either acidic (below 7) or alkaline. Neutral alkalinity is 7. What is ideal for trout and aquatic insects is 7.3 or 7.5, which is also called hard water. Calcium carbonate ($CaCO_3$) from limestone beds and limestone gravel is what makes water hard and ideal for aquatic insects and good fishing. Physical features that can be observed on the surface of the stream are Riffles, Runs, Pools, and Flats. Riffles are very small rapids in relatively shallow, fast-moving water over beds of gravel and rocks that will still hold fish in small depressions in the bottom of the stream (pockets). Runs are deeper and slower parts of a stream, which are usually better for fly-fishing, especially with streamers and nymphs. Pools, slower parts of a stream, are usually over 5 feet deep. Flats are slow, usually wide, shallow parts of a stream that may hold fish at night but seldom in the daytime.

As all of this water moves along its path to the sea, it is interrupted by different obstacles: snags and fallen trees, rocks, large and small, both above the water and under the surface, bends in the river, drop-offs, islands, and undercut banks. There are curves and bends in all rivers and streams. The outside of the bend is a favorite holding basin for trout, since this is where most of the food is being carried by the current. The best fishing position is on the inside of the bend, casting the fly to the outside curve. All of these overhangs and obstructions are excellent cover for fish. Eddies and/or slicks, which you can see behind a rock or boulder and which may or may not be submerged in the stream, are excellent holding basins for trout.

Lakes and ponds are relatively still bodies of water where the fish must be more aggressive in seeking out its food, compared to a stream, where it can hold and wait for the current to bring the food to it. In any event, fish in a lake must have a structure where they can hold for protection from predators and conserve their energy so they can ambush or pursue other fish, shrimp, crawfish, etc., for their food. To read the water in a lake, look for underwater structures, such as logs, large rocks, seaweed, old dock pilings, drop-offs to deeper water, boat wrecks, or points of land jutting into the lake. Lakes are generally much deeper than rivers and streams, so dry-fly fishing is usually only effective at the shallower parts of the lake, where many fish make their nest and larger fish prey on them. Otherwise, nymphs and streamers are the rule for fishing in deeper water. Remember also that lakes, because of their greater depths, have more temperature variations than rivers and streams. Different species of fish will seek out the cooler or warmer temperatures as the surface waters change temperature with the seasons.

Reading the water of brackish and/or saltwater flats and estuaries along our coastlines may be more difficult because of the tides that constantly change the appearance of the shoreline and the water. The tides move and bring food to the fish with each rise and fall of the water level. The same principles apply. Structures, whether dock pilings, coral reefs, old wrecks, or sudden drop-offs to deeper water, make up the hiding places, feeding spots, and resting stations for many species of fish. The time of day, or more important, the time of the incoming or the outgoing tide is most important. It's very helpful to have a hydrographic map, if one is available, with the schedule of the tides for the particular area in which you are going to fish.

FISHING STRATEGY

Based on all of the information gathered from the reconnaissance, an overall strategy can be mapped out for fishing the water. This plan should include the following:

1. The time of day you will start fishing. Many fish, if not most, are crepuscular (more active at dawn or dusk than in the daytime) in their feeding habits. Although many fish are caught in the daytime, if you are after big fish, your chance of success is much better in the evening or early-morning hours. Remember, big fish don't get that way by being dumb.
2. Will you be fishing dry flies, wet flies, nymphs, or streamers?
3. Where will you launch your boat from, or where will you enter the water to wade? Will you be fishing from the shore? If wading, where will you exit the stream?
4. How deep is the water where you will be fishing and/or boating?

5. If you will be fishing wet flies, nymphs, or streamers, at what depth will you be fishing? If fishing near the bottom or mid-depth, will split shot (sinker) be needed, or will the sinking line be adequate?
6. Where will your fishing companions be fishing?
7. Will your fishing companions be fishing flies, nymphs, or streamers?
8. Are you fishing in flies-only water and/or catch-and-release water?
9. What time will you break for lunch or dinner?
10. How late will you fish into the evening?
11. If dry-fly fishing, what hatch are you trying to match?
12. Develop a plan for lunch. If you have a guide, will he or she provide a shore lunch, or should you bring your own?
13. If you are fishing a stream, river, or even a tidal flat, look for "pocket water." Pocket water is the special part of a body of water where the fish will hold for their protection from predators and the best position for capturing their food that is brought to them by the current or tide. Pockets of water are usually at the lee (downstream) side of large boulders or logs, behind pilings of docks, or under shady overhangs of trees and brush at the bends of rivers.

FLY-FISHING TACTICS

1. When you are dressed to fish and have put on your boots, vest, creel, and hat, you must now proceed to the dock or to the point where you will enter the water. Don't forget the sunblock and the insect repellent. This may be a long walk, two or three hundred yards, or it may be short. In any event, carry your assembled rod and reel in your hand or under your arm, with the tip of the rod pointed "behind" you. The butt cap of the rod should be pointing forward along the path you are walking. This is the best way to avoid tangling the rod tip in the bushes, your partner's back, or the ground. Make sure that the fly you have tied to the tippet is hooked on the hook keeper. If you are going to be fishing with a dry fly, make sure that you have sprayed the fly with some good flotation spray. This should be

done at least thirty minutes before you fish with the fly. If you are going to wade, your wading staff should also be helping you make the trip to the stream.

2. After you have all of your tackle together and are ready to enter the stream, test the bottom of the stream with your wading staff first. The first step into the water can be a real surprise if the bottom isn't firm enough to support you. Remember that the depth of the stream will appear shallower than it really is because of the refraction of light through the water. If it looks to be about 1 foot deep, it may well be 2 or even 3 feet deep. Use the wading staff to find out. If you're entering a boat or canoe, first make sure you have on good boat shoes and that all safety equipment is in place, especially the personal flotation vest and cushions for you and your companions. If you're going to fish from a boat, check all boating gear required; and if you have a guide, make sure the shore lunch is onboard.

3. Make a thorough check of all the fishing gear and tackle that you will be carrying with you as you fish (see checklist in chapter 7). Unless you are fishing off the dock in front of your lodge, you will be a long distance away from the supplies and equipment that you might need.

4. Check the water temperature. If the water is too warm (over 75 degrees Fahrenheit), trout will move into the deep holes for the cooler water. If the water is too cold (below 45 degrees Fahrenheit), they will move to the deep holes for warmer water.

5. Watch your casting. Look over your shoulder to see if your loops are tight and your rod is flexing properly, with the line extended on the backcast. Don't try to cast too far. This is one of the most common mistakes made by the novice fly-fisher.

6. If there is no evidence of fish rising to a hatch and you are fishing under the surface of the water with wet flies, streamers, or nymphs, use a strike indicator to help you see a strike. This is especially important if you are fishing for trout.

7. When fishing for trout, bass, or bluegill, a nymph or a streamer may be the only way to catch fish. As most trout anglers know, the biggest part of the fish's diet is made up of nymphs and

other fish (minnows). When not feeding on hatches of aquatic insects at the surface of the water, these fish feed heavily on nymphs under the surface of the water. As much as 85 percent of their diet is made up of such food. These nymphs are the immature stages of the caddis, mayflies, and stone flies that line the bottom of trout streams from early spring through summer and cling to rocks and gravel.

When fishing in these circumstances, you will need a good selection of nymphs, and most important, these nymphs should be small. The hook sizes should be between 12 and 16. Most nymphs are also dark, so your artificial fly should also be dark. The leader should be about 8 feet or 9 feet in length (about the length of the fly rod), tapering down to a 5X or 4X, which is about 2 1/2 pounds of test. About 3 feet up from the end of the tippet, where you will tie the nymph, secure either a split-shot or a lead-wire sinker so the nymph can be carried down near the bottom. This is where the current carries most of the nymphs where the trout feed most of the time. Remember, if they're feeding at the bottom, they're not feeding at the top or even in between. You must get the fly down to where the fish are feeding. How much weight is enough depends on the velocity of the current and the depth of the water. In any event, the total amount of weight should be only enough to keep the nymph down while allowing it to wash freely and naturally in the current. Once you cast the weighted nymph upstream, allow the current to carry it down past you. When the current carries the line into a long sweep, either lift the nymph free and cast it upstream again or slowly strip in the line so you can cast again upstream. A strike indicator (bobber) is not a bad idea, either.

This piece of flannel or cork is usually mounted on the line about 2 or 3 feet above the junction of the leader and the line. When the strike indicator stops moving with the current, give the line a slight tug or pull. You probably have a fish, but don't be surprised if all you have is a weed or a twig. In fact, if you're not catching a weed or two, you're probably not fishing at the right depth. Fairly fast water is what you will want to fish. Remember, this water is like a conveyor belt bringing food to the fish. Shoulders of pools, heads of pools, and long, turbulent riffles behind stumps, logs, and boulders are all holding spots for trout. Wade out carefully and position yourself where the best path for the nymph to run with the current is only a rod length in front of you. With your leader and 4 or 5 feet of line, flip the weighted nymph rig its own length upstream and allow the current to carry it naturally down past you. Just as the current tugs at the line to sweep it out, lift the nymph free and flip it upstream again. Don't let more than a foot or so of your line touch the water. The tip of the floating line can then serve as a strike indicator. When it stops moving steadily with the speed of the current, give it a little tug on the rod tip. You may well have a fish. You may be fishing only a short distance from yourself, but don't be concerned about this. Just stand still and the trout will feed unless you spook them with fast movements or a lot of noise. Even though this kind of nymph fishing doesn't have the spectacular display of fishing dry flies during a hatch, it is a tried-and-true method of catching some big fish.

Once you find a good holding spot, run the nymph again and again through the spot, even though it's only 10 or 15 feet away from you. It is not uncommon for the fish to pass up such an offering many times before taking the fly. Underwater observations have confirmed the interesting practice of a trout in its holding pattern leisurely feeding on nymphs by opening its mouth and letting the current pass a considerable amount of water through its gills and ejecting any inedible objects, such as an artificial nymph.

Natural nymphs are merely passed from the gills to the fish's stomach with little or no change in the holding position of the fish. The gill rakers seine out the edible food from the water as it passes through. Further observations have shown that this method of feeding will go on indefinitely, with the fish rejecting many more inedible debris and objects than the nymphs it will consume. This seems to be nature's way of feeding the fish. The suggestion here is that the artificial nymph should be fished with the lightest leader and tippet you can use and still control your line and fly in the water. Any tippet size under 3X would be difficult to handle. Fish this way while you're waiting for the hatches. Then you can fish on the surface with your dry flies. While fishing this way as you're waiting for the hatch, you may well catch your limit of fish.

Incidentally, this technique is also an excellent way to fish for steelhead. Remember, when fishing for these fish during their early spring or fall runs, you must use the heavier rod and line weights, since the steelhead (rainbow trout) can easily weigh up to 20 or 25 pounds. An 8 or 9 rod with at least 100 yards of backing and the appropriate reel is generally all that is required. These fish can give you a tremendous run for your money. Note: This is also the same tackle to be used for saltwater fishing.

CHAPTER 8

The Kind of Fish the Fly-Fisher Fishes For

If you are going to fish with a fly rod and tackle, it's important to know what kind of fish you are fishing for and most likely to catch. If you have never fished before or have never fished with artificial flies and a fly rod, it's very helpful to know some of the different fish you can catch by fly-fishing. Most neophytes associate fly-fishing with fishing for trout and let it go at that, but fishing for trout is only part of the fly-fishing challenge. Along with fishing for trout in designated trout waters (which is an experience in itself), the opportunities are almost limitless for catching everything from panfish, bass, and even northern pike in freshwater rivers and lakes to snook, bonefish, and even tarpon and sailfish in saltwater oceans. For anyone who is just beginning with a fly rod, fishing for panfish or bass in a small lake is an excellent way to learn the ropes about fly-fishing and have a lot of fun while learning!

PANFISH

The panfish in North America include bluegill, sunfish, crappie, rock bass, and even an occasional perch. Smallmouth and large-mouth bass are most often larger than panfish and generally much more aggressive, but don't underestimate any of these fish as a challenging sport on fly rod and tackle. Occasionally, a walleye or even a northern pike or muskie (muskellunge) will take a streamer fly or a popper (a floating fly that pops when pulled in the water), and even though this doesn't happen often, your fishing skills and tackle should be prepared for such an onslaught so that you don't lose hook, line, and sinker or even your rod and reel from such a strike.

Figure 20. Essential parts of a fish

Fish are cold-blooded, with body temperatures about the same as the water of their habitat. Most fish are covered with scales. Some are covered only with skin without scales. Fish reproduce by the female laying eggs in the water (sometimes by the millions) that are then fertilized by the males dropping their sperm (milt) on the eggs. Fish have the senses of sight, taste, smell, hearing, and touch to help them.

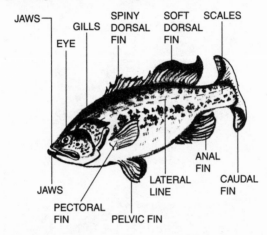

Eye. Most fish have monocular vision. Each eye sees separately for a wide view.

Spiny dorsal fin. This fin is used for balance and to protect the fish from enemies.

Soft dorsal fin. This fin is used for balance and for forward locomotion.

Caudal fin. Used for swimming, especially for a fast thrust of speed.

Anal fin. Used for balance and for swimming.

Lateral line. This organ senses sound and movement in the water. Like another ear.

Pectoral fin. Used for stability and steering with some locomotion.

Pelvic fin. Used for steering and stability.

Gills. Respiratory organs used for breathing.

Jaws. Strong bones with teeth so that the fish can grip its prey and ingest food. Food is not chewed but ingested whole. Digestion occurs in the stomach.

Figure 21. Popular fish for fly-fishing

Salmonidae (Trout)

Black Bass (Smallmouth)

Panfish (Bluegill)

Saltwater (Bonefish)

All of these freshwater fish are generally classified as "warm-water" fish, since they are quite active in lakes and streams with water temperatures ranging from 65 to 80 degrees Fahrenheit. If anything is important to fishing, it's the temperature of the water. Temperature controls the life of the fish and the fish's food from start to finish. If the water near the surface gets too warm, the fish will most often move to deeper and cooler water. Water that gets too cold will not only discourage fish from feeding, it will also restrict the food supply of aquatic insects, crustaceans, and minnows. Although the fish does not hibernate, in very cold water (below 50 degrees Fahrenheit) it becomes inactive and feeds very little. In addition, the food that the fish feeds on is very inactive and even dormant at low temperatures. Watch the temperature of the water to make sure the fish are biting.

Bluegill *(Lepomis macrochirus)*

The sunfish family, and especially bluegill, are found in almost all sections of the United States. In the southern part of the country they are called bream, most often pronounced "brim." In the North these fish grow about 1 inch a year and reach 5–6 inches in three years. In the South they grow much faster. Bluegill prefer quiet, weedy water where they can hide and feed. The larger fish prefer deeper water but move into shallow water to feed in the morning and the evening. The food of the bluegill consists of terrestrial and aquatic insects and some vegetation. These fish generally feed in the daytime and can grow to as much as 2 1/2 pounds! The best time for these fish in the northern latitudes is late May or early June, when the water temperature rises to about 67 degrees and the fish begin to spawn in the shallow waters with sand and gravel bottoms. The fish will build a dishlike nest in the sand and gravel and then guard it with fighting fury. This panfish is a formidable adversary on a fly rod with light tackle. With water temperatures in the sixties or low seventies, artificial wet and dry flies are especially effective. With warmer temperatures, poppers with yellow and white combinations are very effective with a No. 10 hook. These fish can be very spooky at times. Use 4-pound or even 2-pound test leaders at least 6 feet long.

Black Crappie *(Pomoxis nigromaculatus)*

Crappies, one of the most popular panfish, are carnivorous and feed on many natural baits; but their preference is for small minnows. Therefore, fishing with the fly rod, streamers, very small spinners (small metallic blades that spin when pulled in the water), poppers, and wet flies with split-shot (small lead balls split to fasten to the line) sinkers are recommended. Crappies don't seem to mind cloudy water and most often run in schools. When you catch one, stay in the same spot to catch your limit. Hooks should be Nos. 10–6 and the leaders, 2–6 pounds. These fish can grow up to 4 pounds.

Yellow Perch *(Perca flavescens)*

This popular member of the Percidae is also known as a ringed perch, striped perch, and jack perch. It is a lake fish for the most part, although it can also be found in streams and rivers with cool, clean water and sandy or rocky bottoms. It's a favorite in many gravel pits. Its color can vary somewhat, but generally the body is yellow, with a white belly and dark green on the back and with six or eight dark green bands down the sides.

Although this common member of the panfish family is not rated as a top-notch game fish, it ranks near the top, and for some people it is the top, a gourmet delight. Today this fish can be found in almost every state in the United States and can be taken with hook and line with almost any kind of lure or bait, including nymphs and even dry flies. These fish usually weigh in the neighborhood of 1/4–3/4 pound, but occasionally a whopper can be caught in the 1–2-pound class. The female will drop her spawn in the cover of weeds and brush in water 3–4 feet deep. The males accompany the female during this spawn and will immediately eject their sperm to fertilize the eggs. As much as one-half the eggs will hatch into fry in two to three weeks. The young perch will then stay in the weeds for protection from predators feeding on insect larvae and plankton. They grow very slowly, with a high mortality rate, but they have still managed to prevail all over the country except where the commercial fishermen have depleted their ranks. This fish is a magnificent adversary on a fly rod and offers the neophyte fly-fisher an excellent opportunity to sharpen his or her fly-fishing skills at the closest lake or pond where there is fishing for panfish. In addition to developing your fly-fishing skills, the other rewards are that this fish is one of the best entrées for the table.

Walleye *(Stizostedion vitreum)*

The walleye is the largest member of the perch family. It is often called a "walleyed pike," or even a pickerel, but it is not a pike or a pickerel at all. It can grow as large as 20 pounds, although the most common catch is in the 1–3-pound class. A catch of 6–10 pounds is in the trophy class. The fish are so delicious to eat that one doesn't see too many trophies of this fish on the wall. This freshwater denizen of the lakes prefers cold water, that is, less than 85 degrees Fahrenheit, and is rarely found in rivers or streams. Fly-fishing for this fish is best done with nymphs and streamers, which imitate baitfish, since minnows and other fish make up most of their diet. Since fish are more cautious during daylight hours—when they are most exposed to predators—the best time to fish is the evening (just after sunset) or at night. These fish travel in schools, so if you catch one, others are holding nearby and at the same depth. Most of the time these fish hold near the bottom of the lake. When fishing at these depths, watch the line very carefully for any lateral or unusual movement and strip (retrieve the line by hand) the line back in with very slow strips. The walleye takes its food very slowly, and the hook must be set the moment the fish takes the fly or it will reject it. Unfortunately, this fish, too, has been depleted by commercial fishermen with gill nets, but where it is still available, it is one of the finest game-fish catches the angler can ever make.

BLACK BASS *(MICROPTERUS SPP.)*

Black bass offer a special challenge to the fly-rod angler. Biologists now recognize eleven varieties of this species of fish, but as a practical matter, the angler is only concerned with two categories, the largemouth bass and the smallmouth bass. All of these fish are also classified as warm-water fish. The largemouth seem to prefer warmer waters (65–75 degrees) than the smallmouth. No matter where you're at, though, up North or down South, don't look for the largemouth in the mountains, where the water temperatures might fall below 65 degrees.

Largemouth Bass (Micropterus salmoides)

The largemouth bass can always be distinguished from the small-mouth bass (aside from having a bigger mouth) by the upper jaw and lip, which in the largemouth extends back behind the eye when the mouth is closed. In the smallmouth, the lip extends only to the posterior margin of the eye. Remember, though, that colors and markings can vary depending on the local habitat and the age of the fish, but the upper lip locations should be definite. The largemouth is generally larger than the smallmouth, and in waters of the southern United States may reach as much as 20 pounds. In the northern part of the country these fish tend to be smaller, and a trophy size would be in the neighborhood of 8–11 pounds.

The largemouth is a voracious feeder and a superb fighter on fly-rod tackle. It will usually "attack" the fly or popper with a single gulp, so the hook must be set (imbedded in the jaw of the fish) immediately. It is not unusual for these fish to leap right out of the water when they are fighting the hook. Be prepared for lots of action with these piscatorial denizens of the lily pads and backwaters. The best fly rods to handle the large poppers are 7 1/2–9 feet. The largemouth prefers the quiet waters of lakes and slow stretches of rivers. They hide out in the waters around stumps, logs, docks, and weed beds. Early in the season they will be found in shallow water, but as the water gets warmer, the fish will move to the deeper, cooler water.

Smallmouth Bass (Micropterus dolomieu)

The smallmouth bass is smaller than its cousin the largemouth. The smallmouth can reach 9 pounds, but 1–5 pounds is more common. This fish is generally found in cooler water, on rocks, stone, or gravel beds, but weed beds, logs, and other structures are also very popular. In the spring and again in the fall the smallmouth is found in shallow water, especially in spring, when the fish are spawning. In the summer they will move to deeper holes and cooler water in the lakes and rivers. This fish will put up a fierce battle trying to shake the hook, and pound for pound it puts up more of a scrap than its cousin the largemouth.

Fly-rod tackle for the smallmouth should use 4–10 pound test leaders (nearly invisible nylon line) and tippets with Nos. 4–8 hooks for the streamers (wounded minnows) and poppers. This bass is not leader-shy (frightened by the sight of the line), but the leader should be about the length of the rod for the beginner, and smaller tippets, 4X or even 5X, should be used for the small flies and streamers. Experienced fishermen will often carry two or three reels with different fly lines for the different fishing conditions they might encounter. Those who are just starting to fish with a fly rod should start with a floating weight-forward line (front 30 feet of the line heavier than the rest of the line) with appropriate backing (additional line attached to the fly line), leader, and tippet, and when fishing nymphs or streamers (which are always fished underwater), they will add some split shot (lead weights) to carry the line and leader to the required depths of the lake or river.

The smallmouth feeds on almost anything that moves and will often strike a lure (artificial wood or plastic minnow), popper, or fly with a violence that will startle even the most experienced fisherman. It is not uncommon to find fish almost as big as they are in their stomach. When the smallmouth is "small," it will feed on aquatic and terrestrial insects, crayfish, and minnows. Depending on the time of year for their hatches, they will also feed on the larvae and nymphs of these insects. As the smallmouth increases in size, much more of his diet will be made up of larger minnows (streamers), frogs, crawfish, etc., and of course, worms. Streamer flies, of course, resemble minnows or small eels, and poppers may simulate frogs, crawfish, or even mice. When the smallmouth is lurking in the shallow water early in the season, even a well-placed dry fly, such as the Adams or any mayfly that is hatching, will also prove very productive. These flies— the streamers, nymphs, and dry flies—should be tied to a No. 4 up to a No. 10 hook and fished at appropriate depths. Dry flies and poppers, of course, must be fished at the surface if that's where the fish are feeding, but nymphs and streamers should be fished at depths where the fish are feeding or just hanging out.

Remember that these fish will strike even when they have a full stomach!

TROUT *(SALMONIDAE FAMILY)*

Trout is the name given to certain members of the Salmonidae family and is one of the most sought after fish with fly rod and tackle in North America, or for that matter, the world. Today ichthyologists struggle with the classification of the various trout because of the differences in habitat, temperature ranges, and hybridization of these fishes. As a practical matter, for someone just starting to fly-fish, the salmon, the rainbow, the brown, and the brook trout are the major challenges for fly-fishing. True trout, including the rainbow and the brown, are almost always spotted black. The brook trout, which is really a char, never has black spots.

Trout are much more sensitive to water pollution and water temperature than any other freshwater fish. Whether in lake or stream, water temperature must be carefully measured to avoid fishing futility. If the temperature is too cold, below 40 degrees, the trout do not feed much and are very lethargic. If the water is too warm or polluted, or both, the fish will starve for oxygen and cannot maintain their normal metabolism. Trout have the highest oxygen demand of any of the freshwater fishes. With temperatures over 83 degrees Fahrenheit, the trout will suffocate and perish. When water temperatures get this high, the trout will seek out cooler water in deeper parts of the lake or stream and/or in deep holes under logs and underneath shady banks of the stream. Ideally, good trout water temperature is between 45 and 65 degrees Fahrenheit.

Trout are probably the easiest to startle of all the fish, and this is undoubtedly one of the main reasons they have survived as well as they have up to this time. This is especially true of the trout that live in the rivers and streams. These waters are generally more shallow than the water in the lakes and the oceans; and in shallow water the vulnerability of the trout (especially the big ones) to predators, such as eagles, owls, hawks, osprey, herons, ducks, seagulls, cormorants, and kingfishers, is very great in the daytime. Raccoons, otters, bears, and bobcats will also take one of these fish anytime the opportunity presents itself. The cormorant, as big as a goose, is said to be able to eat its weight in fish in a day!

The trout, like most all other fish, has an additional sense of hearing, with its "lateral line" running from its gill to its tail or caudal fin, on each side of its body. This lateral line picks up any vibration from any predator, including man. Don't underestimate this acute sense of hearing. Even a clap of thunder from a rainstorm or the clunk of a rock from a fisherman's boot in the water will spook feeding fish into hiding. Because of these conditions, the mature trout is very unforgiving of any mistakes or carelessness by the fisherman. Any loud noise, even a sloppy cast or the sudden movement of a heavy shadow over the stream, will send all fish under cover in an instant. Be quiet if you want to catch fish, especially big fish!

Although the smaller fish will feed during the day on hatches and other aquatic food, night feeding is the preferred time for the bigger fish. This is especially true of aquatic insect hatches on the surface of the stream. During the daytime these larger fish will remain hidden in deep holes, under logs and bank overhangs, or any other structure where the cover is good and the velocity of the water is low. The large fish will feed during the daytime, but they will seldom feed at the surface. Their preference at this time will be underwater food, such as aquatic insect nymphs, larvae and pupa or crustaceans, aquatic plants, and most importantly for big fish, minnows or small fish. Aquatic insects spend most of their life cycle underwater. They surface to hatch and mate for procreation, lay their eggs on the water for reproduction, and then die. This entire life cycle of the insect, from eggs attached to stones on the bottom of the stream to larvae and nymph and finally to the surface for the wings to dry (dun) and then rise up into the atmosphere (spinner) to mate and then die, may be as short as two months or as long as four years, but it is generally about one year.

For the angler just starting fly-fishing with fly rod and tackle, it is very important to understand how these fish live, what they eat, how they breathe, what their environment is, who their enemies are, and their habitat. Selecting the right fly rod and tackle and, of course, the right fly to satisfy all of these conditions and challenges for a particular fish, is the essence of fly-fishing. Although luck is always important, the more skill and knowledge the angler has, the more fish will be taken.

Rainbow Trout *(Salmo gairdnerii)*

The rainbow trout, *Salmo gairdnerii* (the new name is *On-corhynchus mykiss*), is native to North America and one of the best game fish in the world. It lives in the lakes, streams, rivers, and even the oceans ranging from Southern California to Alaska. These fish, originally native to the Pacific coastal waters, have now been introduced throughout the United States. Rainbows that live most of their lives in the ocean or the Great Lakes but spawn in the rivers and streams along the coast are called "steelheads," or "bows." The steelhead grows much larger than the rainbow that lives in the small lakes, rivers, or streams. They may weigh as much as 20 or even 25 pounds. One of the most distinguishing features is the reddish band along the sides of the body, but the rest of the spots and colors may vary considerably, depending on habitat and time of year. Although all trout must have colder water than other freshwater fish, the rainbow can tolerate warmer water (up to 83 degrees Fahrenheit) than the other species of trout. In addition to being excellent food for the table, this fish is highly prized for the fight it puts up and the way it leaps up out of the water to shake the hook. On a fly rod, even a 1-pound rainbow is dynamite.

Brown Trout *(Salmo trutta)*

The brown trout, which is a native of Europe, is found in streams from the Mediterranean to the Black Sea watersheds and as far north as arctic Norway on the Atlantic and Siberia on the Pacific Rim. This fish was first introduced from Germany into North America in the Pere Marquette River of Michigan in 1884 by a German named von Behr, hence, the name "German brown trout." Shortly afterward, in 1885, it was introduced into California from Loch Leven, Scotland. In the western part of the United States this fish may still be called the "Lock Leven" trout. Since that time it has been introduced all over the world. The brown has more tolerance of warm water than the brook trout but slightly less tolerance than the rainbow, with temperatures over 83 degrees Fahrenheit being fatal. The ideal temperature for the brown trout is 50–65 degrees Fahrenheit. This fish is one of the best trophies the fly fisherman or fisherwoman can bring to the net. Some anglers believe that the brown is more difficult to catch than either the rainbow or the brook trout, and this may be one reason that some browns become quite large and prey on other trout. Another very important characteristic is the tendency of this fish to prefer slower-moving water; and if the food supply is good, he will remain in this neighborhood indefinitely. Watch the deep holes close to the bank and the big logs in the stream. This fish is very spooky, especially in the daytime.

The color of the brown is generally a golden brown with large black spots on its sides, back, and dorsal fin. These spots are usually surrounded by a halo of a lighter shade than the body. The underside may be either yellow or white. The appearance of the brown trout is very much like the landlocked salmon in the United States. The only major difference is in the vomerine teeth of the fish. The teeth of the brown are better defined and developed. Brown trout found in the Great Lakes or other large lakes as well as the oceans will also resemble landlocked salmon, since they become very silver in color and are spotted black. The brown trout has been known to reach 40 pounds (from the big lakes or the ocean), although anything over 10 pounds is considered a trophy. Most of the fish caught with a fly rod in a trout stream weigh less than 2 pounds. The record on rod and reel for the United States is 31 1/2 pounds, from the White River in Arkansas in 1972. The brown is also a voracious feeder, with both aquatic and terrestrial insects making up a substantial part of its diet. The larger fish will also eat frogs, mollusks, crayfish, and most importantly, other fish! The larger fish are almost entirely piscivorous (eating only other fish). But when the annual hatches of the large mayflies (*Hexagenia limbata*), caddis flies, and stone flies occur, these fish will readily gorge themselves at the surface. The brown is very active at night, and most of these larger trout are caught after dark. Many anglers, if not most, believe that this is the most difficult trout to catch on an artificial fly.

Brook Trout *(Salvelinus fontilalis)*

The brook trout of northern North America, which is really a char, is truly native to the United States and Canada. The chars are one of the two main divisions of the salmonids and are distinguished by the arrangement of teeth on the roof of the mouth, called the

vomer, and the absence of any black spots, although there are usually small red spots bordered by pale blue aureoles on the sides of
the fish. The brook will also have very vivid colors, with marbled,
wormlike markings (vermiculation) on its back. Although this fish
may live in large rivers, lakes, and even oceans, its most well
known habitats are small streams and brooks throughout most of
North America. Most fish caught in these small streams are less
than 10 inches long. Brook trout in the big lakes or the ocean may
reach over 5 pounds, but this is unusual. The record is 14 1/2
pounds.

The brook trout is a very active, aggressive, and strong fish that
feeds on aquatic and terrestrial insects, minnows, and crustaceans.
Although the larger fish are definitely piscivorous, they will very
often show a preference for insects, especially during the insect
hatches of mayflies, stone flies, and caddis flies as well as terrestrials, such as ants and grasshoppers. According to many anglers, the
"brookie" is their favorite quarry with a fly rod. These fish are very
sensitive to water temperature and prefer to feed in water of 40–55
degrees Fahrenheit. The lethal limit for these fish is about 77 degrees, which is less than for any other trout! They probably have the
highest oxygen demand of any freshwater fish. The logging, paper,
and mining industries have sadly reduced the number of these fine
fish to the point of extinction in many parts of the country.

One anomaly of the brook trout is that the greater the fish population in a given stream or lake, the smaller these fish will be, 4–6
inches. As the population of this fish diminishes, mostly from natural predators, not polluters, the fish get larger! Stocking the lakes
and streams, therefore, would seem to feed the predator pike fish
and reduce the size of the trout. Biologists and ichthyologists are
working continuously to solve this problem and hopefully will
come up with some answers for more and bigger brook trout.

Steelhead

The steelhead is actually the anadromous form of the rainbow trout.
At one time it had its own classification, but today it is identified by
the scientific name *Salmo gairdnerii,* the same as the rainbow trout.
Its native range is the Pacific Coast and its tributary rivers and
streams from northern California up to Alaska. By virtue of its in-

troduction into the Great Lakes, it is now common in most all of the streams and rivers draining into the lakes. These fish are one of the finest game fish that the fly-fisher will ever meet on river or stream. They are magnificent fighters and can easily reach weights of 20 or even 25 pounds. These fish spawn in the rivers and streams draining into the big waters of the ocean and/or Great Lakes. They then enter the big water and may not return to the river to spawn for one to two years. In the ocean these fish will feed on small fish, squid, and crustaceans. In the Great Lakes they will feed on alewives, smelt, and other fish. There are two runs each year, one in the early spring and the other in the fall. The spring runs produce smaller fish, and the larger fish are caught in the fall runs. The holding area of these fish in the streams is not the same as it is for other trout. Most of the time they will seek out water where they can rest after their struggle upstream from the big water. They will find ledges and pools just above rapids or in more quiet channels on their way upstream. Unlike some salmon, the steelhead will feed on various kinds of insects while migrating upstream to spawn, although spawning takes priority over feeding. With this knowledge, fly-fishers now use nymphs and even some terrestrials, along with a single salmon egg of different colors. Even dry flies are now being used on some rivers, although the nymphs seem to be the most popular. Fly-fishing equipment for these big fighting fish is in the heavyweight class, with rods as long as 9 or 10 feet, handling 9- and 10-weight line. Weight-forward tapered lines are the best, and lines lighter than 8 weight should not be used. Since these fish may make very long runs, 150–200 yards of 30-pound backing should be used with adequate reels that have good adjustable drags. Steelheading is an outstanding challenge for the fly-fisher, and once the novice masters some of the basic fly-fishing techniques, this challenge offers one of the most memorable fly-fishing experiences.

PACIFIC SALMON *(ONCORHYNCHUS)*

Of the six species of Pacific salmon whose range is from Alaska to the California coast, only two are really important to fly-fishing. These are the chinook (or king) and coho salmon. Imported into the Great Lakes not long after World War II, these two species of very aggressive, large, and delicious fish have added more to the sport of fly-fishing since the introduction of brown trout to North America in the nineteenth century. These important fish have declined on the Pacific Coast because of overfishing by commercial and Native American fishing along with pollution and dam building for electric power.

These anadromous fish must spend an important part of their life in freshwater rivers and streams to reproduce. When the young return to the deep water of the ocean or the Great Lakes, they will spend two years or more growing to very large sizes, such as 12–40 pounds, before they return to the rivers and streams where they were born so they can reproduce. Pacific salmon spawn (reproduce) once and then die. During this reproduction migration, they rarely feed but will strike an artificial fly if properly presented on the stream. When these fish reach two or three years of age, the large males will often develop a hook (kype) on their bottom or upper jaw.

This kind of fly-fishing can only be done on the rivers and streams during these migratory runs in the spring and fall. Most significantly, presenting the fly to these fish requires a very different technique than with trout fishing. And most importantly, heavier tackle is required to hook and land these large fish. In between river migrations, they are fished in the oceans and lakes with artificial lures following the thermoclines (water temperature levels) at depths of 50–200 hundred feet.

ATLANTIC SALMON *(SALMO SALAR)*

This well-known member of the Salmonidae family ranges along the North American Atlantic Coast from Greenland to Cape Cod. It is one of the favorite fly-fishing quarries for sport fishing. The young remain in the freshwater streams from one to five years and then migrate to sea, reaching maturity at three to five years. The mature males will develop a hook (kype) on the jaw. Unlike Pacific salmon, these fish may spawn two or three times during their lifetime. They are one of the strongest fighting fish found anywhere. They may leap out of the water 3 or 4 feet when hooked or struggling up a rapids or waterfall during migration. Only heavy tackle should be used with these fish. Their average weight is about 12 pounds, although they may be much heavier. The big difference in fishing for salmon compared to trout is that salmon migrating in rivers and streams do not feed. Why they strike an artificial fly is still a mystery, but they do, and these flies are quite different from the standard flies used for trout and bass. These fish are also some of the finest eating fish from the sea, but pollution and commercial and Native American overfishing have decimated their population to dangerous levels. According to some authorities, the species is now threatened. Catch and release as well as flies only are common requirements on many North American streams.

AMERICAN SHAD *(ALOSA SAPIDISSIMA)*

This anadromous fish is a member of the herring family distributed along the Atlantic Coast as far south as the St. Johns River in Florida. They range in weight from 1 pound to as much as 10 pounds. Because they are good fighters, they are a favorite for fly-fishing. They are fished primarily in the relatively shallow tributary rivers and streams along the coast during their annual migrations. They have also been popular along the West Coast since their introduction in 1871 into the Sacramento River.

SALTWATER FISH

Saltwater fly-fishing includes so many circumstances and conditions that are different from freshwater fishing that it might even be called a unique sport all its own. The enormous variety of fish and many saltwater tidal basins, estuaries, inlets, and rivers affected by the tides would seem enough to classify this sport as definitely different from fishing in fresh water. However, the principles of fishing with fly rod and reel are still the same! The tackle should be different to cope with the saltwater conditions, but it doesn't have to be to get started. Knowing some of the most popular fish and their habitat will be a big help getting started.

Saltwater anglers started fly-fishing in the 1930s in earnest and for the most part caught tarpon, snook, and red drum. Later on they added bonefish, sea trout, permit, and barracuda, all of which would take a fly and were very strong fighters. What has made salt-water fly-fishing much more popular in recent years has been the substantial reduction and/or control of commercial fishing along with the corresponding resurgence of fish populations, such as the redfish or channel bass in the South and the striped bass in the North. Along the intercostal waterway of Sarasota, Florida, even the pompano and the red snapper are now plentiful due to the re-striction of commercial fishing in these waters. Not only are there more of these fish today compared to twenty years ago, but they're also easier to get to from the major urban centers along the coast. Some of the most popular fish along the southern coast and the Gulf of Mexico are:

Bonefish *(Albula vulpes)*

This is one of the most popular fish that anglers seek in the saltwa-ter shallows of warm seas. They are rarely caught north of Miami, Florida. They are most active on a rising tide, feeding into the tide or into the wind. Although they are often fished from a boat with a guide, wading is very popular on the shallow flats. These fish aver-age 3–4 pounds, and it is not uncommon for them to reach 5 or 10 pounds. They can reach 20 pounds. Among the best flies for this fish are the bucktail and polar bear streamers. The marabou streamer is also very effective. Hook sizes range from No. 6 to No. 1/0. Bonefish swim along the bottom and are seldom near the sur-face (except when the tide is out and the water is very shallow).

Spotted Sea Trout *(Cynoscion nebulosus)*

This is one of the most popular saltwater game fish in the southern United States. These fish are not really trout or from the family Salmonidae, but members of the drums, family Sciaenidae, and re-lated to the weakfish and the croaker. It's also called speckled trout or simply trout. This fish is usually caught within a hundred yards of the shore unless the water gets too cold; then it will move to deeper and warmer water. Streamer flies are the best lures, and the bigger fish will put up a stiff fight. One hundred yards of backing would not be too much. These fish are normally about 4 pounds, but 7–8 pounds is not unusual. A world record is 15 pounds 3 ounces. Speckled trout can be caught at any time of year, but the spring and fall are the best times. This fish is excellent for the table.

Red Drum *(Sciaenops ocellatus)*

This fish is more often known as "redfish" or "channel bass." It is a bottom-feeding fish that feeds mostly on crustaceans and mollusks. This fish can be spotted moving along shallow, grassy bottom flats as it starts feeding on a rising tide. When feeding this way, its waving tail may be seen just breaking the surface of the water. When this happens, the angler can present just the right fly for this feeding fish. The most conspicuous mark of identification of the red drum is the black spot on the base of the tail. Fish of 1–6 pounds are common, and some up to 40 pounds are not uncommon. The record weighed 83 pounds and measured 4 feet 4 inches. The small fish, fewer than 15 pounds, are very good eating. The larger fish are coarser.

Barracuda *(Sphyraena barracuda)*

This long, slim-bodied fish resembles a great northern pike and is very common in the American Atlantic from Florida to Brazil. They are very aggressive and will generally attack any flashing object in the water. The inshore varieties are smaller than their cousins in the deep water, which can reach up to 100 pounds. The smaller fish close to the shores are more likely to be in the order of 3–5 pounds. A long cast and a very fast retrieve are needed with this fish. The fish will put up a magnificent fight, but the food value is questionable at best.

Some of the more popular saltwater fish along the shores of the Atlantic in the northern part of the United States are:

Striped Bass *(Morone saxatilis)*

This is one of the most exciting fish to catch on any tackle, but especially with a fly rod. It is also known as a greenhead or a rockfish (south of New Jersey). Fishing in the spring and fall is the best. This fish is excellent food for the table, and it is believed that the

Plymouth colonists were able to survive in the summer of 1623 with this plentiful supply of fish. In 1670 the first free school in the New World was financed by the sale of striped bass within the colonies.

The striped bass will average 5–10 pounds, and it is not uncommon to catch them at 30 pounds. They can reach 70 pounds. They range along the coast of the Atlantic from Maine to Florida and along the Pacific Rim from Oregon to Monterey, California. Stripers are anadromous, since they migrate from salt water up freshwater rivers. They are often found in fresh and brackish waters, with a preference for bays, deltas, and estuarine waters. They roam the surf, flats, and rivers that empty into the ocean.

Atlantic Bonito *(Sarda sarda)*

This very fast moving small tunalike fish is actually a member of the mackerel family. It is most frequently found in offshore waters as far north as Massachusetts between August and October. Bonitos are most plentiful in the summer and can weigh up to 15 pounds, although 3–6 pounds is average. Large schools of bonito sometimes feed in inlets near shore. These speed demons can strip 150 yards off your reel before you've had time to think about it.

These are some, but certainly not all, of the popular saltwater fish that can be taken with a fly rod and fly. They are described here because of their wide distribution and popularity. There are many more, including, but not limited to, the regal tarpon, snook, ladyfish, crevalle jacks, amberjacks, and even sharks. All of these, and many more, are found along the inshore waters of the eastern coast. As noted before, the big bill fish, such as the sailfish and the marlin, which may weigh up to 500 pounds, are caught today on heavy fly rod and tackle along the Gulf Stream and the Caribbean and in the warm waters of the Pacific Coast.

FISHING QUALITY, QUANTITY, AND CONSERVATION

Although fish, like many other members of the animal kingdom, face many threats to survival, by far the most pervasive problem is the destruction of their habitat and commercial fishing. Of all the conventional usages and practices of modern society that affect our environment, one of the most destructive, as far as fish are concerned, is the farming and development of land in the watershed of our rivers, lakes, and saltwater tidelands along the coast. Any pollution that reaches the streams and lakes by means of agricultural irrigation, fertilizers, and/or pesticides, with the storm-water runoff, along with the sediment, sand, and topsoil that washes into the water, completely destroys the insect food and oxygen supply required by the fish. Aquatic insects, which are a primary food supply for the fish, cannot thrive and reproduce when gravel beds are covered with sand. In addition, clean gravel beds are essential for many of the female fish to deposit their eggs on. Today all of this habitat is threatened and in many cases is in serious jeopardy. Much of it has already been destroyed.

Commercial fishing on the lakes and the high seas has depleted some of the species stocks to the point of extinction. The highly mechanized and computerized equipment even uses satellite tracking to locate many of the fishing beds. Some of the nets are over a hundred miles long, and many of the factory ships, which do the freezing and canning, are subsidized by different countries fearful of unemployment. This industry is almost completely unregulated and highly politicized because of the international makeup of the fishing fleets. The future supplies of salmon, steelhead, brown trout, and many saltwater species are definitely at risk with commercial fishing.

CHAPTER 9

The First Fly-Fishing Exercise

To learn fly-fishing, you must start fishing. With preparations and basic training now complete, it's time to begin. To become more familiar with all the new equipment and develop some of the basic fly-fishing skills, it's a good idea to start with some of the fishing waters and fish that are easiest to catch. Going for bluegills is not only an excellent way to learn the use of a fly rod and tackle; it is also a lot of fun. Bass are in the same water as bluegill and can add considerably to your experience with the fly rod and also a lot of excitement to your first fly-fishing exercises. Fishing for cold-water trout with your fly rod is one of the best fishing experiences any angler could ever have. The true magic of fly-fishing will be revealed with this new piscatorial adventure. For any one of these fish, the first task is to find where they are located and where they are feeding. The second task is to understand the etiology or life cycle of the fish and how they function in their environment. The third task is to present the proper fly that will result in a strike!

BLUEGILL ON THE FLY ROD

The first assignment is to start fishing for bluegills. Bluegills and their cousins the sunfish and pumpkinseeds are found in warm-water lakes, ponds, and rivers almost everywhere in America. As soon as the ice thaws in the lakes in the northern part of the country, these fish move out of the deeper water, which is warmer, to the more shallow water—1–10 feet closer to the shoreline. In the southern part of the country these panfish are called brim; but wherever you find them, they are fun to catch with a fly rod. Look for these denizens of the shallows in cover that is very near weed beds, lily pads, around docks or logs, and especially at the drop-offs, where the shallow water meets the deeper water. One modification of this generalization would be the spawning season in late May and early June, when the fish build nests in the sand and gravel beds of the lake shallows near the shore. Early in the season the fish are feeding on small minnows and aquatic insects. At this time, use small streamers, nymphs, or wet flies. Later in the season, when the water reaches temperatures over 68–70 degrees Fahrenheit, surface poppers (floating lures) and dry flies work better. The best times to fish are the early morning or evening, although these pan-fish can be caught at any time of day. These fish will respond to a variety of surface and sinking flies and poppers, so have a good selection available when you start fishing. Small popping bugs of red and white combinations, yellow or yellow and black and black and white, along with rubber spiders, wooly buggers (caterpilars), and nymphs of black or brown colors will make up an excellent selection. Floating flies or poppers are the most effective when the fish are holding near the surface or as deep as 4 feet. Tackle up with about a 6-weight system, with a weight-forward floating line of a bright color and a 7 1/2-foot 3X leader of 6-pound test.

The mouth of a panfish is small, so make sure the size of the hooks are in the 10–14 range. A good way to begin is to fish from the shore or in a boat near the shore. There's no need to wade unless you want to try out your new boots.

To start fishing, pick out a target in the best cover you can see (polarized glasses are a big help) and then strip out about 20 feet of line off the reel. While you are doing so, wiggle the tip of the rod to take the line through the guides and onto the water. With all of this line lying on the water in front of you, use a roll cast to straighten out the line; then pick up the rod tip and lay down a regular forward cast. Put the fly or popper next to or just inside the fish cover, that is, lily pads, weeds, or logs. After you cast the fly on or over the cover, bring the tip of the rod down toward the fly. Then begin to retrieve the fly, rubber spider, or popper by stripping (drawing) the line back with the left hand and running the line over the forefinger of your right hand, which is gripping the rod. Don't get a four-finger death grip on the line while you're retrieving. The death grip is a poor habit to get into and can only cause you problems when a fish strikes. Strip in the line and pause. Strip fast and sometimes strip slow. This type of retrieve is trying to suggest a wounded insect, minnow, or grasshopper.

When the fish strikes, it is important to set the hook as fast as you can before the fish realizes that what he has is not edible and spits it out. Most of the time, bluegills suck in their food—flies, nymphs, etc.—the same way that you suck on a straw for your cola or iced tea. To set the hook, raise the rod tip up gently but firmly. This action will set the hook! Hold the rod tip up to maintain pressure so that the fish can't throw the hook. All fish will head for cover when they realize that they are hooked. If they are faster than you are and get into the logs or the deep weeds, you not only will lose the fish but also some of your tackle as well. When you see the fish head for the weeds or under the dock pilings, point the rod up and away in the opposite direction and then continue to retrieve the line with your left hand, slowly but firmly, until you're ready to net the fish. When retrieving the fish from the net, wet your hand and lift the fish by grasping him headfirst to avoid being spiked by his fins. Remove the hook with long nose pliers or forceps and put the fish in your creel if he is of legal size or back in the water if he is too small.

If you have no luck with your fly or popper at the surface after you have thoroughly gone over the entire area of fish cover, change colors and/or flies and try a different level of water. Fish may be feeding at a lower level. Try a sinking fly. Retrieve your cast slowly by stripping in a few inches at a time. Pause, then strip in again. If the slow retrieve doesn't work, try a fast retrieve to trigger a strike, just as you did with the surface fly. If still no strike, try a new location or a new feeding level. If you are trying a new feeding level, you may change spools on your reel for a sinking line or just add a split-shot sinker to your leader on the weight-forward line. If still no strike, try again later in the day or evening. The lake or pond may be too busy with boaters and swimmers.

FLY-FISHING FOR BASS

Black bass have a wide range of habitat in the United States and can be found in almost every state of the union. They are classified as a warm-water fish inhabiting large and small lakes, rivers, reservoirs, and farm ponds. The two most prominent members of the family are the largemouth and the smallmouth bass. They favor water temperatures of 60–80 degrees Fahrenheit and will favor the same type of cover as bluegill or other panfish. The largemouth prefer the warmer waters; the smallmouth, the cooler water. Fly-rod tackle for bass should be a little heavier than the tackle used for panfish. A 7 1/2-foot rod designed to cast a 7- or 8-weight fly line is a good choice for the heavier bass bugs. Even a 9- or 10-weight line might be desirable for the heavier fish, that is, anything over 5 pounds. The weight-forward bass-bug taper is about the best bass fishing line for delivering heavy flies and poppers, especially in windy conditions. The floating line should be used when the bass are feeding at the surface or just below the surface. Try this line first. When fishing below the surface, use a sinking line, such as a wet tip. These lines cast well and can be used effectively for casting streamers, floating bugs, muddler minnows, etc. Using a 4-to-5-foot leader with a popper, deer-hair bug, or muddler minnow, work the surface first, then let the sinking tip pull the fly deeper into the water. Then retrieve it with a strip-and-pause crippled-minnow action. As with the bluegills, if the slow retrieve doesn't work, try the fast retrieve. The leader tip and tippet should test at about 8 pounds for small- to medium-size flies (10–4-size fly hooks.) Conventional dry flies imitating mayflies, caddis, or grasshoppers work well along with the poppers and floating bugs. For diving flies that imitate crippled minnows, frogs, or water snakes, use the flies that will dive when retrieved and float when you pause.

The same casting technique you used for the bluegill can be used for bass fishing. Select a target in the fish cover, strip out about 20 feet of line onto the water, use a roll cast to straighten out the line, and then use a standard overhead cast to place the fly on the target. Keep the rod tip low as you retrieve the fly by stripping the line back through the rod guides. Introduce some action to the fly with the line stripping. Try to keep the rod tip pointed straight at the fly as you introduce this action to the fly. When a bass strikes, the action is much stronger than the hit of a panfish. With the larger and much tougher mouth, the bass will try to kill its catch with its severe bite. Setting the hook requires much more force than what is needed for a trout or a panfish. Drive the hook home with a rapid upward thrust of the rod tip and make an extra pull on the line with your line hand to make sure of the hook's penetration. As soon as you feel the weight of the fish on the line, pull on the line to set the hook again, and even again if the fish is especially large.

If the fish is large, anything over 5 pounds, and is putting up a stiff fight, you should be sure to give him as much line as he can carry as long as you maintain constant pressure on the line. At this time you should be fighting the fish from the reel and not from the line in your hand. As soon as possible, the slack fly line between the stripper guide and the reel should be reeled up. Bass seldom run far like a steelhead when hooked. They prefer to run for cover, twist, dive, turn, and jump to throw the hook. They are very strong for their size. When the fish is tired and you have brought him close to you or the boat so you can land him, try, if possible, to grasp him by the lip so you can lift him and retrieve your fly. If your grasp is firm, the fish will be paralyzed but not harmed, and you can easily lift him from the water. If this retrieve is too inconvenient, use your landing net. With your rod tip raised, bring the fish toward you. With your net hand, move the net under the fish and then raise it to bring the fish up out of the water. Put the rod under your arm while you extract the hook from the jaw of the fish.

FLY-FISHING FOR TROUT

If you have raised your confidence level for fly-fishing by fishing for panfish, you may now be ready to fish for trout. Here again the angler should follow the same plan that was used when fishing for panfish and bass. Find the best location for the fish and where they are feeding (pocket water), the temperature of the water, how the fish are behaving in their particular environment, and what is the best fly presentation for the fish. One of the best ways to begin fly-fishing for trout is to start with a local trout farm where these fish (mostly rainbows) are raised commercially and the public is invited to fish from the ponds during certain business hours. Usually no fishing license is required, and the fish are hungry most of the time. No boots are needed, and you can fish from the shore of the ponds. There is plenty of room for practicing your casting, presentation, and retrieving of the fish. Most of the farms will even clean the fish for you, and you will have the satisfaction of bringing home some good fish from your first fly-fishing experience. Incidentally, these fish are ecologically very sound. The food and water used for raising these fish are carefully monitored for quality control, and there is practically no danger of contamination from the agricultural or industrial-waste runoff that has become a problem in some rivers and trout streams. For the fly-fisher who is approaching a trout stream for this first experience of fly-fishing, the stream should be studied to discover the location of the best lies (cover) for the trout in the stream. The river operates like a conveyor belt, bringing food to the fish 24 hours a day. The trout will hold in a "lie" to conserve energy waiting for the right selection of food to be delivered by the stream. These lies are in the quieter parts of the stream (pockets), which may be behind submerged logs, boulders, or overhangs of the stream banks.

Along with this reconnaissance, the feeding level of the trout can be estimated. If the fish are feeding at the surface, a careful observation of the stream will usually show the dimples in the water where the fish are taking the hatches. Many times the fish will even expose themselves at the surface while gorging themselves on a particular hatch. If the fish are feeding on a hatch, it is very important to determine what insect is hatching and attempt to match that hatch with your selection of artificial flies. The most common surface hatches will be either one of the mayflies, the caddis flies, the stone flies, or terrestrials, such as the grasshoppers. If there is no activity on the surface, then the trout are feeding below the surface. Remember, except in very cold weather, when the metabolism of fish is greatly reduced, the fish are always feeding. It's also important to remember that the fish are always facing upstream, since this is where the food comes from. When the fish are feeding below the surface, you must determine what level they are holding at below the surface. They may be just below the surface, at mid-depth, or at the bottom. If the water is only 4 or 5 feet deep, it is relatively easy to find the subsurface feeding level. If the stream is much deeper than 5 feet, some experimentation may be required to find the right level. Remember, when trying out different split-shot sinkers on your leader, the velocity of the stream is a major factor in determining how fast the fly will sink. Strip out more line to get the streamer or nymph down to the bottom and work the retrieve slowly when you strip the line in to keep it there.

When selecting a fly for your first fishing cast and you are not real certain what hatch is out for the surface-feeding fish, try an Adams No. 10–16. This is part of the old rule When in doubt, use an Adams. If you are fishing under the surface of the water for the first time, try a Wooly Worm size No. 6–12. Try different colors. This fly has an excellent history of success. If you are fishing nymphs, try a Hares' Ear in size 6–18; or if you start with a Muddler Minnow (wet fly), use size No. 4–12. These flies have a very impressive record of success. Many times just changing colors will make the difference between success and an empty creel. If you are using a No. 6 system with a weight-forward line and a 9-foot 4X leader, any of these flies should work well.

If you are fishing with dry flies, cast upstream. This is the best way to get a drag-free float for your fly. Trout will usually reject a dragging fly that doesn't look natural. When making an upstream presentation, spray the dry fly with some flotation material. Make short casts upstream of 30 feet or less and let the fly and the line drift back to you with the current. As the fly drifts back, strip in the line that has drifted back with the current and shoot the line out on your next cast. You don't want any slack line on the water between you and the fly. Set the hook fast when a trout strikes and you will avoid spooking the fish with surplus line lying on the water in front of the fly. If there are no strikes, move forward a few steps so you can present the fly to new holding areas. Move slowly.

If fishing under the surface, attach a strike indicator to your line. This small piece of putty or flannel that will float on the surface will help you see when a trout is striking your fly or nymph. Allow 3 or 4 feet plus the tippet length between the nymph and the strike indicator or allow two times the depth of the water between the nymph and the indicator. Cast upstream and strip in the surplus line as the current carries the fly and the line back toward you. Watch the indicator. The slightest movement sideways usually means a strike, and you must set the hook immediately or the trout will spit out the nymph. To imitate minnows or sculpins (small baitfish), make your presentation downstream with a Muddler Minnow or a Wooly Worm. Set the hook with a quick, smooth movement. Move the rod tip up and maintain steady pressure to tire out the fish so you can bring him in. Don't horse (pull the line too fast) him in too fast or he will break the tippet and you will lose him. Work the fish upstream from you so you can bring him gently up to your net or your free hand and lift him from the water and remove the hook. If you are releasing the fish, be sure to face him upstream and allow him to regain his equilibrium before you release him.

STREAM FISHING

For many fly-fishers a stream is an ideal place to fish. It offers beauty, variety, excitement, and accessibility. For many situations, a boat is not required, and the stream can be fished either from the shore or by wading. The stream must first be studied to identify all of the possible holding areas for the fish. Considering all of the stream craft lore, a choice must be made of the best fly to begin with, the time of day or night to start fishing, and where to start fishing.

Streams can be highly complex. No stream has a perfectly uniform and even bottom or a constant velocity of the current from bank to bank. Logs, rocks, sandbanks, and changes in direction along with the change in the gradient (steepness) direct the flow of a stream. Each curve changes the flow from one bank to the other.

Each one of the rapids aerates the water, and each pool slows down the current. It is among all these variable conditions that the fish will be holding to protect themselves from predators and catch fresh food. The current acts like a conveyor belt, constantly moving food to the waiting fish. To accomplish this, the fish will almost always be facing upstream, against the current. The fly must therefore be presented upstream from the fish so that it can move with the current downstream to the waiting fish.

Many pools holding fish in a stream are formed on curves, which means that the main flow of the current, sweeping around against the outside of the curve, has worn itself a deep channel against the bank while gravel has gradually built up in the back eddy on the inside of the curve. The water around the outside of the curve is an ideal holding place for the fish. Runs of this kind also occur from time to time on straight stretches of the river when gravel beds, boulders, or logs force the current into a narrow flow that will cut into the bank to form pools for the feeding fish.

Frequently, trees and bushes will hang over these pools, offering additional protection for the fish and helping to keep the temperature of the water down. Wherever these pools occur, they will catch the eye of the angler. Watch out for high water or low water for any given time or stretch of water. These conditions can change from year to year and from season to season. When these changes occur, some of these pools will disappear, and new ones may appear.

Wading is an important part of stream fishing. It should be done with caution to avoid spooking the fish and compromising personal safety. It's important to avoid sending out unnatural ripples ahead of one's wading and equally important to avoid making underwater sounds by stumbling over rocks or logs. Wading provides tremendous advantages, but they can be nullified by spooking the fish with too much noise and/or disturbance in the water. It is wise not to be too ambitious in wading until one has built up a good measure of experience and confidence. Currents can be deceptively strong; round boulders can be slippery and treacherous; loose gravel may slip away under your feet in a heavy current; and don't forget that the easy wade downstream may end up in deep water over the chest waders and the return journey, against the stream, will not be so easy. In any event, don't forget the wading rule: under all conditions, place one foot down very securely before moving the other foot. This is the best assurance for safety, and it also means that all movements will be slow and deliberate, as they should be in approaching fish. It's a good idea when starting to wade to find both the place where you will enter the stream and the place where you will exit it. Don't be cavalier about this chore. Backtracking in a stream against the current can be a real struggle.

A staff is almost mandatory for anyone who has not waded a stream before. Wading staffs of all descriptions are available commercially from almost any fly-fishing sporting-goods store, but a good stout rake handle will also do the job and can be had from any hardware store and for less cost than the collapsible staffs at the sporting-goods store. If you do use a rake handle from the hardware store, be sure to drill a 1/4-inch hole at the top of the staff and attach a leather thong strap through the hole so that you can grip the staff through the leather thong as you would a ski pole when you are skiing. When fishing the stream, it's helpful to think of the stream from the point of view of the fish. Although it's hard to consider a fish as doing much thinking, there is no question that fish do react to any stimulus in their environment. If flight is their reaction to danger, pursuit is their reaction to food. The pursuit may be very active, as when the prey is a small fish or a fly that looks like one; or it may be calm and deliberate, as when the fish rises to a drifting mayfly. Most important, the mechanism of this reaction is built into the fish. That's how the fish survives and sometimes reaches old age.

When fishing, it is the feeding reaction that you are trying to stimulate with the presentation of your dry fly, wet fly, streamer, or nymph. If a hatch is suspected, a dry fly will be presented in an attempt to match the hatch on the stream. Without a hatch, the wet fly will be presented at different depths and speeds, looking for the combination that will trip the reaction of the fish and get a strike. Whether fishing with a dry fly or an underwater nymph, it is not unusual to cast as many as twenty-five or even thirty times from the same spot to the same target before a strike. Patience is needed along with frequent observations and changes of fly patterns to get the fish to react to the presentations. Obviously, accurate casting is a big advantage in this kind of fishing. With more experience, the angler will soon be able to identify those pockets that have produced the most strikes with the most success. Although one can't argue with success, don't overlook the other stream pockets for what they have to offer. In the final analysis, fish are where you find them. A good fly-fisher respects the rules because they make sense most of the time. But good fishing also requires that these rules be varied from time to time to accommodate the fish.

LAKE FISHING

If your first fly-fishing experience is on a lake, there are some important differences between lake and stream fishing that should be understood. Compared to most streams, lakes for the most part are very deep, and fish that move into these greater depths for cooler or warmer water will always conserve their energy in their search for food. A fish will rarely, if ever, rise from a 20-foot depth to take a dry fly. However, it is not uncommon for that same fish to move into water that is 2–10 feet deep to not only feed, including a hatch of flies on the surface, but to spawn in the spring of the year. These same fish will also move to the mouth of streams and creeks that empty into the lake for the food supply that is washed in from these feeder streams to the lake.

Some lakes have shallow, firm-bottom shorelines or long, gravelly points and bars that favor wading. These lakes are a delight to fish by wading, but the fly-fisher must be ever so careful, since these conditions can change very rapidly with drop-offs, muck, and marl (loose clay) bottoms and weeds. In any event, if you are wading, check the basic conditions of the lake before you enter. First measure the temperature of the water at the depth you will fish. Next, observe how the wind is blowing. Remember, as the sun rises in the sky, the wind increases. The least amount of wind is at dawn and sundown. If possible, plan your route where you will be wading in the lake so that the wind will be favorable for fly-casting. If you can be sheltered by trees on the shoreline, so much the better. If you can estimate where the drop-offs occur from the shallow to the deep water, that is the place to fish for the larger fish. Closer to the shore the fish will be much smaller. Panfish make up most of the fish population in these shallow waters, although it is not unusual to encounter a larger fish on occasion.

If you are fly-fishing a lake, chances are you will be fishing from a boat from time to time. In practically all of these cases you will be with a companion, or even two. Casting will now be different from fishing in a stream, where you are almost alone when you cast your line. Generally, you should cast at right angles to the length of the boat. If you are at the stern end of the boat and you want to cast ashore, cast with your right hand. Your companion fishing from the bow of the boat will cast left-handed or over the left shoulder to avoid the fly lines being tangled. When one or the other fly-fishers gets a strike and says, "Fish on," the other line must be reeled in to avoid line entanglement. This can easily happen if the fish on the line makes a run at the boat in its attempt to shake the hook. Unless you are fishing dry flies on the surface of the water, your nymphs, streamers, and wet flies will be fished below the surface. The task is now to get the fly down to the level where the fish are holding and/or feeding. Generally, this can be accomplished only with some split shot attached to the line. This split shot should be attached about 3–4 feet above the fly on the leader.

When stripping the line in on your retrieve, you will probably collect some seaweed. If you don't do this, you aren't getting down to where the fish are. Be sure and clean off the weeds from the fly.

Although you can fish from a boat from an anchored position very well, it's a good idea to move the boat with the oars very slowly along the shoreline, casting from the boat toward the shore. If the wind is just right, the boat can drift along the shoreline without the use of oars. The drift can even be slowed by the use of a sea anchor or just dragging the regular anchor. Cast downwind ahead of the boat and don't forget to strip the line fast enough to keep the fly line straight and avoid bends. If you cast upwind, the line will be easier to keep straight and control when the fish strikes.

A dry fly is very effective on a lake, in the spring as well as in the summer months. Poppers and spiders are good on a light leader, and hair flies are always reliable for panfish and even a large bass if the fly is large enough. The larger fish will come to the surface for the larger flies. Use a No. 10 or even a No. 6 fly for these larger fish. Under calm conditions it is a good idea to cast the fly out, let it sit briefly, then begin working it back to the boat with short strips that alternatively drag it and rest it. Dry and wet flies will often take fish right next to the edges of weed beds or standing reeds. Bass are commonly taken among lily pads, and on occasion a pike or pickerel will take a popper from this cover.

A problem with fishing from a boat on a lake is "boat noise," which will spook the larger fish. Vocal conversations generally have no effect underwater, but any thump on the hull of the boat from heavy footsteps or repositioning tackle boxes, oarlocks squeaking, and of coarse, outboard engines in the vicinity of the boat will. Swimmers and other recreational boats can also be a problem for the fly-fisher. If there is too much of this kind of traffic, you will have to move to a new location.

CHAPTER 10

Saltwater Fly-Fishing

Sooner or later, most fly-fishing neophytes will try their fly rods in salt water. And why not? There are thousands of miles (estimate is over ten thousand) of saltwater coastline in the United States, and the fly-fishing opportunities present unlimited challenges and superb sport. Most important, this fly-fishing bonanza is not reserved for the experienced angler only. The novice has only to learn and apply the principles of basic fly-fishing in freshwater streams and lakes to the new saltwater bays, estuaries, flats, surfs, and ocean reefs. These saltwater conditions are different from freshwater conditions, but even though saltwater conditions are different, the principles of basic fly-fishing techniques are the same as for fresh water. This new experience in fly-fishing will bring most satisfactory rewards as well as a lot of fun. If you are just starting fly-fishing in salt water, you can even begin with the same equipment you used in fresh water. If you do use this equipment to start with in salt water, be sure that you wash it with fresh water after each use to avoid corrosion problems. If you continue with saltwater fly-fishing, you should investigate the use of saltwater fly-fishing equipment. Catching these heavier fish (fish well over 10 pounds) on lightweight tackle can devastate your lightweight tackle and ruin your fishing day.

The new saltwater fly-fisher has to learn that saltwater fish are very different from freshwater fish. First of all, there are many more varieties of saltwater fish than there are of freshwater fish (see Fig. 22 for some typical varieties). Except for the occasional surprise that has taken your fly, this great variety should not cause problems. Incidentally, because the variety is so great, an excellent addition to the angler's list of accessories and equipment is a small handbook on the identification of saltwater fish with pictures. If possible, get a handbook that also tells you about the fishing sea-

---

Figure 22. Typical saltwater fish

GRUNTS

Small shallow-water fish caught by anyone using an imitation (epoxy fly, crab or shrimp fly imitations) with a fly rod. Retrieve the fly with short 4-inch strips. Most hits will occur after each strip when the fly is in a free-fall condition. This saltwater fish is one of the most popular catches for the angler just starting to fish in salt water as well as the experienced fly-rod enthusiast.

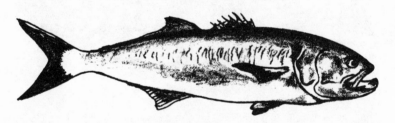

BLUEFISH

Excellent game fish for anyone with a fly rod. This fish is found all along the Atlantic Coast from Connecticut to Florida. Very sharp teeth, so a 40-pound tippet is needed. Since this fish moves in toward the shore to catch baitfish, a feathered streamer pattern in white or combinations of white and yellow or red that imitates these baitfish should be used. The retrieve should be very quick.

Figure 22 continued

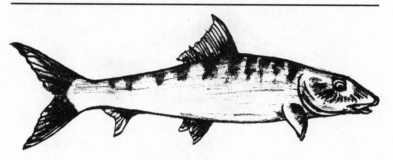

BONEFISH

This is one of the most popular fish for anyone fly-fishing the shallow flats where you can actually see the fish trying to catch crabs, shrimp, or small baitfish. Light tackle is the usual order of the day since the fish range from 5 to 10 pounds. Use 1/0–6 flies, depending on the size of the fish. This fish ranges from Florida and along the Gulf coast to Mexico.

STRIPED BASS

These large fish (5–20 pounds) range along the Pacific and Atlantic Coast, from Oregon to San Francisco and Maine to the Carolinas. Streamer flies imitating baitfish are most common. Because baitfish are mostly white, white must be the dominant color for the flies. Hooks should be 3-0–5-0.

sons and the time of the tides when these fish are running in that part of the ocean in which you are going to fish. Nothing is more disappointing than to find out that you should have been there six weeks ago, when the fish were running. Remember the rule Don't fish in empty water. Another difference between freshwater fish

Figure 22 continued

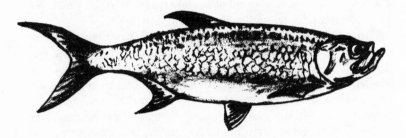

TARPON *(Megalops atlantica)*

These saltwater fish can get very big (from 50 to 150 pounds is not un-usual) and when they do, they present a real challenge to the fly-rodder. Light tackle just won't do for these fighting fish. They will dance on their tails on the top of the water when fighting the hook. They frequent fairly shallow and brackish water all along the coast from Hatteras to the Keys and along the Gulf coast down to Panama. The extremely hard mouth requires that the hook be driven home very hard, not just once but two or even three times, to be sure that the fish is hooked. The hooks must be very sharp or the fish will be lost. Use 3/0 or 5/0 hooks with at least 150 feet of 25- or 35-pound test line (Nos. 12–13-weight lines) and various colored streamer flies, with white the dominant color.

and saltwater fish is that the latter rarely, if ever, feed on or near the surface. There are exceptions to this rule, of course; but as a practical matter, if you are starting to fish in salt water, you will be fishing below the surface.

One of the most important differences between freshwater and saltwater fishing is the influence of the tides anywhere along the coastal waters of North America or any other saltwater coastlines. Tides have little or no impact on freshwater fishing, but saltwater fishing is an entirely different matter. The tides not only affect the elevation and, of course, the depth of the water you will be fishing, but also, most importantly, the tides have an immense impact on the feeding habits of saltwater fish. The magnitude of the tide varies depending on the location and/or latitude of the coastline where you might be fishing. What is important to understand is that the tide is bringing food to the feeding fish, whether it is an ebb tide (moving out) or a flood tide (moving in). The exception to this is when there is no tide, or what is known as a "stand," which is a time between tides when there is no tidal flow.

To get started in salt water, try your freshwater tackle on any one of the small saltwater creeks, inlets, bays, and anywhere else you might have access to some salt water. In most of these cases, you will have your feet on the ground, but if a small boat is available, so much the better. One of the best ways to begin saltwater fly-fishing is to wade the shallow flats in the many tidal basins of the coastal waters or fish from the many public piers, causeways, and even the bridges. Just be sure your backcast won't encounter any road traffic, especially if you're fishing off a bridge or causeway. If you are using the fly rod and line that you started with in fresh water, for example, an 8-foot-6-inch No. 5 rod with a WF No. 5 or No. 6 F line and 7-foot knotless, tapered 5X leader, you should do well fishing in these inshore waters for small grunts and croakers. Don't be surprised if they talk back to you when you land them. You don't need a boat and you don't even need waders to start salt-water fly-fishing in many places along the Atlantic, Gulf, and Pacific Coasts. Many fishing piers, some of them quite elaborate, provide extensive accommodations for the angler. You must have all of your own equipment, although some bait stores on the piers will rent chairs, fishing tackle, and bait. The most important thing to consider when saltwater fishing anywhere is the timing of the tides. Both ebb tides and flood tides provide good fishing; but in each of these situations, the magnitude of the tidal current varies from a minimum to a maximum. The stronger tidal current, of course, provides more food for the feeding fish. The feeding fish will position themselves at feeding stations to reap the benefit of the food moved toward them by the tides. Many of these feeding stations are next to bridge pilings and caissons as well as the public fishing piers. The tidal currents completely reverse direction every seven hours. You can obtain a schedule of these tidal movements from most sport shops and/or bait shops along the coast. Shrimp are the food of choice for most of these fish, so the angler with a fly rod should use a fly that imitates these shrimp. However, since these fish feed well below the surface, the rig with the imitation shrimp fly should be tied to a leader and barrel or three-way swivel with a split-shot sinker attachment so that the fly will lie at the level where the feeding fish are holding. Larger saltwater fish, such as a redfish or a snook, will also feed on any available baitfish, so a streamer fly, such as the Clouser's Minnow, a Deceiver, or a Seducer in red and white and orange or yellow, should be used. Since so many baitfishes are white, flies with a predominant white color are most often favored. If you have a good chance of catching these larger fish, be sure to check your leader and tippet for the proper strength and make sure that the tippet matches the fly you are going to use. Many of these saltwater fish, such as a barracuda, have very sharp teeth and are also stronger than most freshwater fish. For many of these larger fish, a 40- or even an 80-pound wire shock tippet is recommended. Check with the local bait shop in the area in which you are going to fish for the right leader and tippet.

Once you have become acclimated to fishing in salt water, you will want to explore the many other challenges that this exciting sport has to offer. Since most saltwater fish are heavier and stronger than freshwater fish, light tackle just won't do it; heavier equipment will be required for any fish on the line over 10 pounds. Most professionals recommend a line-and-rod weight of about an 8 or 9 or even 10 for beginners or anyone else. This combination should handle any fish weighing less than 40 pounds. The novice should be able to cast this line as far as 50 feet. For most fishing along the coast, a rod 9 or 9 1/2 feet long should be adequate. According to most professionals, this weight rod should use Nos. 4–2 flies. The reel must be able to resist salt water. Any part or component of the reel that is not resistant to salt water will quickly corrode and breakdown. A good saltwater-resistant reel will also be able to provide excellent service for freshwater fishing when fishing the anadromous steelhead or salmon. In addition to this important feature, the reel must also have adequate capacity and a very good drag. Many fish have been lost because a drag on a reel was set either too tight or not tight enough. The minimum capacity of the reel should be no less than 200 yards of 20-pound. Dacron backing plus the entire fly line. When you start fishing for heavier fish and you are using a No. 10 line or heavier, the backing should be changed to at least 30-pound test. If this kind of fishing is a good possibility, a separate spool with these weight lines might be the best bet.

One of the most popular fly lines for saltwater fishing is the WF-9-F-SWT (weight-forward, No. 9 weight floating saltwater taper) or a WF-9-F-BBT (weight forward No. 9 weight floating bass-bug taper). The leader should be compatible with the flies that you will be using and should be at least 8–9 feet long. Check on your extra tippet material to be sure that the tippet is the same test and diameter as the leader tippet. To avoid frustrating problems with your line and leader, make sure that the leader and its tippet are no longer than the length of the rod. Although longer leaders are often recommended for some very clear water conditions, 95 percent of the time the added length is only surplus and will cause problems by wrapping around the rod on the forward or backcast.

The outfit made up of a 9 or 10 rod with a saltwater reel that has a smooth drag and capacity of 200–300 yards of backing along with a 9-foot tapered leader will provide you with a wide range of fishing capability. If you are beginning on any of the saltwater flats along the coast, casting with this line and leader combination should allow the fly to be fished at almost any depth up to 4 or 5 feet deep. Saltwater flies are very different from the common mayflies, caddis, and stone flies most often used for freshwater fishing. The most common and probably the most popular saltwater flies are the streamers, which imitate the baitfish and the nymphlike flies imitating shrimp. Shrimp are practically the universal food of saltwater fish. Colors are important because of the changing water conditions of clarity, turbidity, ebb tide or flood tide, and wind, but in any event, be sure that your fly selection includes several white patterns. White is the most common color of the baitfish and is one of the easiest colors to see when casting out or in the water. The Bonefish Special is one of the more popular flies in the last few years, especially for the bonefish, although an occasional permit or even a barracuda might take this attractive fly. Poppers and some of the dry flies are also good on occasion and shouldn't be overlooked. Be careful about the size of the hook. The hook should be compatible with the tippet test you are using and for the novice should be the lightest and smallest you can use for the fish you are after. A big problem with many of the smaller fish is a hook with wire that is too thick. A streamer on a 1/0–3/0 hook 3–4 inches long would be just fine for redfish or sea trout and even a bonefish, but for fish over 10 pounds or 5 feet in length, like the tarpon or any billfish with very hard mouths, these hooks would probably be inadequate. When making your fly selection, it's a good idea to check with the local sporting-goods shop or bait shop for the best fly for the fish you're after.

When fishing the inland saltwater bays, flats, and inland waterways in the waters of the Gulf and southern part of the East Coast, the main game fish will be sea trout, snapper, pompano, snook, tarpon, redfish, mackerel, barracuda, bonefish, and an occasional shark. There are many other fish in these waters, but these are the common and popular ones. A boat is a big asset but not a necessity in these waters, since fishing will be in and around the shallow bars and islands. Cast up close to the mangroves, grass beds, and sandbars, where most of these fish are hiding, waiting for baitfish. Use your long streamer flies, alternating with different colors and different rates of retrieve, just as you did with the freshwater streamers, and fish with the ebb tides or flood tides. Most fish caught in bays are seasonal residents. In winter they migrate to deeper, warmer offshore waters or move southward. Among the common fish caught in the bays and lagoons of the Gulf coast and the Atlantic are striped bass, bluefish, pompano, snook, tarpon, grouper, weakfish, croaker, and flounder. Popular bay fish of the Pacific are king salmon, kelp bass, rockfish, croaker, grouper, and flatfish. In these bays, as in other waters, fish concentrate where they find food or cover. Bare bottom areas are poor places to fish. On an incoming tide, many fish gather just inside the inlets, especially where a current forms an eddy that holds the food organisms. On the outgoing tide, the fish move through the pass and feed outside, at the edges of the bars and eddies. Flats along the shore and in the coves are best near high tide, when fish range into the shallows to feed. Steep shorelines are most productive on a high, falling tide. Channels are usually best at low tide, when fish leave the flats.

Oyster or mussel beds, in water 3–12 feet deep, are feeding grounds usually good on any tide, as are the kelp beds along the West Coast. Grass flats with water 4–6 feet deep also attract many kinds of bay fish, as do rocky bottoms. Where fish lack natural cover and feeding grounds, artificial reefs have been created by wrecked automobiles and other junk. These spots are usually marked with buoys to make them easy to find. No matter where you fish, though, check the tides. Generally, the better fishing will be during the last two hours of the ebb tide (going out) and the first two hours of the flood tide (coming in). Sometimes fish will be difficult to find. When this happens, try smaller flies, such as size 12 or 14, which will be taken much more readily than the larger sizes. In any event, it's never wise to spend too long in one spot without some sort of response, nor is it wise to pass up unlikely water without a few trial casts, as fish are nearly always moving.

Flies should be the No. 8 to the No. 2, with the smallest size being for the shallow flats when the water is calm. The weedless flies will avoid a lot of annoyance and are very effective. Always use a floating line in these waters, and when wading, move very slowly, since these fish spook easily. When retrieving, strip the line in with short strips of 2–3 inches. Remember that the best anglers spend most of their time studying the water and moving to the best position, as opposed to constant casting. Random casting and/or noisy wading will only spook unseen fish.

To use flies effectively, it is helpful to understand some differences between freshwater fly-fishing and saltwater fly-fishing. Most saltwater fly-fishing is done in situations where moving currents are either very weak or absent altogether. In these situations, all of the fly's action comes from the hands of the angler. This is essentially a matter of allowing the fly to sink to the desired depth, then retrieving the line in small strips, from an inch or two at a time to as much as a foot or so for many of the larger fish. The most important factors seem to be the length of the strip and the speed of the strip. Some fish seem to want a long, very slow but deliberate rate of retrieve, and other fish react more quickly to a fast darting motion of the fly. What the fly is trying to imitate is a real baitfish that is trying to escape from the predator. The depth of the fly presentation is especially important in the flat water flats. If the water is 5 feet deep and the fly is presented at only 1 or even 2 feet beneath the surface, the fish at the 4- or 5-foot level will ignore the fly.

Saltwater fish seldom feed on the surface. It is necessary, therefore, to cast the fly for a subsurface presentation. Since there is no current to move the fly, as you might have in a river or a trout stream, the fly must be stripped in fairly fast to prevent the weighted fly from sinking to the bottom. For some fish, such as a ladyfish, the line must be stripped in very fast or the fish will ignore the fly. Stripping the line rapidly in from a successful cast can soon become an arduous task if repeated cast and retrievals are unsuccessful. Change flies and rest your arm if this is the case. Some fly-fishers even use a "stripping basket" to help with this chore. The basket is especially useful if fishing while wading the flats or in the surf.

Fishing the surf, causeway shorelines, piers, and bridges is also productive in any of the waters of the Atlantic, Pacific, or Gulf, but to really improve your chances of success, carefully check what fish are running and the best time of the day to fish them. Kingfish, snook, and especially mackerel, make for some of the best saltwater fishing on light tackle; but with rare exceptions, they are only available during their seasonal runs. The time for these runs varies not only with the fish but also with the location on the coastline. Along the more northern coastlines of the Atlantic, some of the most popular game fish are the striped bass, the sea trout, the red fish, and the false albacore. The Clouser Minnow is one of the most popular flies. Check the local bait shops for the most timely information.

Piers provide the saltwater fly-fisher with access to deep water and also furnish cover for fish. A pier that juts out from a sand beach may be the only shelter for fish along miles of open beach. Piers commonly shelter schools of baitfish that attract passing schools of bluefish, mackerels, and other game fish. Barnacles encrusted on the pilings entice such fish as sheepshead and porgies. The deep end of the pier is not always the best, however, for fish feed near shore many times, especially when the breaking-wave action keeps the plankton and other food animals stirred up. Night fishing is also popular, since game fish come to feed on the baitfish that are attracted to the lights. The fly-fisher must use extra caution on the piers because of other anglers nearby.

Bridges and causeways over and across salt water are very good for fishing for sheepshead and many kinds of snappers and grunts. Bluefish, mackerels, weakfish, and croakers move under the bridges regularly as they follow the flow of the tide to feed. On moonlit nights game fish such as snook, tarpon, and striped bass will gather on the up-tide side of the bridge to prey on shrimp, minnows, and other bait animals that congregate just in front of the shadow of the bridge.

Fishing the deep water off the ocean reefs and the waters of the Gulf Stream for the big marlin or sailfish with the fly rod has become more and more popular in recent years. This fishing requires much heavier equipment for the bigger fish in these waters and in most cases requires the services of experienced guides.

The angler who wishes to tackle these larger fish should become more advanced and experienced with light tackle before trying for this big game.

Once you have developed confidence fly-fishing in fresh water, try salt water; it has a magic all of its own, and you'll love it! It can provide the maximum challenge, but more importantly, it's a lot of fun.

CHAPTER 11

After You Catch the Fish

After you have done everything you are supposed to do to catch fish with a fly rod and an artificial fly, the first fish you catch may come when you least expect it. If it's the first fish you have ever caught or it's a special trophy fish, it could be a big surprise. If you have fished before with more conventional tackle, you may also be impressed with the action and the challenge you must cope with to land your fish with this lightweight rod, floating line, and artificial fly. But what does one do when the tired fish is finally brought to the net? At this time, the successful fly-fisher is confronted with several options and major decisions that will require different actions, depending on the actual circumstances when you are fishing. The following options may fit the occasion:

1. Release the fish. The fish is either too small or the angler is following catch-and-release rules in effect for the water that is being fished. In any event, if the size of the fish is below the legal limit, smaller than the angler wants to keep, or has to be released because of the catch-and-release rules, care must be taken if the fish is to survive the fishing struggle and the trauma of the catch. If you know ahead of time that you are going to release the fish, do your best to set the hook as soon as possible to catch the fish on the lips and prevent the fish from swallowing the hook.

    Once the fish is brought to within reach of your hand and/or the net, the first thing to do is to grasp the fish either by the tail or around its girth with one hand and then remove the hook with the other hand. If the fish is a black bass, you may grasp the fish by the lower lip of the mouth with the thumb and forefinger. The removal of the hook can be done by hand, but if the angler uses a pair of surgical forceps (your standard equipment hanging from your fishing vest), this removal of the hook avoids injury to the fish and is much faster and more efficient. The removal is especially easier if the hook is a barbless hook, which is used by many trout-stream anglers. In most cases, the hook will not permanently harm the fish. If the fish is to be returned to the water, wet your hands and grasp the fish under the belly. Then, while holding the fish, gently place the fish in the water and hold it there until the fish regains its strength and can swim away under its own power. If you are in a stream or a river, the fish should be held with its head facing the current. Do not just throw the fish back into the water. The fish will probably die with such rough treatment.

2. Keeping your fish. If your going to keep the fish, temporary storage is immediately required. If you can't keep the fish alive and several hours will pass before it can be filleted or prepared for cooking, remove the entrails and the gills to prevent spoilage. If you have a creel, either a wicker or a canvas one, put in layers of wet moss or seaweed to keep the fish fresh until it will be gutted. The fish should be good for up to two hours without removing the entrails if the weed bed is kept wet and the temperature does not exceed 70 degrees Fahrenheit. A fish can be kept for several hours this way as long as the temperature is not too high.

Cleaning your fish. You may want to put on a pair of thin plastic gloves that can be disposed of when the fish are cleaned. These gloves are available at any hardware store where paint is sold and are very inexpensive. Make sure your fishing knife is sharp. A dull knife will only result in frustration and spoil the fish. To gut the fish, hold it by the tail and slit the belly of the fish from the rear vent to the head. To avoid piercing the entrails, don't make this slit too deep. There is a membrane between the abdominal cavity and the backbone close to the backbone. Cut this membrane carefully to expose the blood line and/or the kidney. Next, completely open the chest and abdominal cavity by cutting from the head to the tail. Then reach into the chest cavity near the esophagus and pull out all of the entrails with one movement. Dispose of the guts in an old newspaper or garbage disposer. When gutting the fish, remember to wipe the inside cavity of the body surface clean of all blood vessels and be sure to remove the kidney. The tip of a teaspoon is very good for this job. The guts and the kidney spoil very fast in a dead fish. It is the guts, kidney, and blood vessels that give the fish a poor taste. As soon as the fish is gutted, it should be set in ice, refrigerated or frozen, if possible.

Never bring a fish home for your spouse to clean. The quality of freshness will disappear (and probably spoil the fish) with the long trip home, and the quality of the marriage relationship will also deteriorate. Future fishing trips may also be jeopardized.

Other ways to temporally store a fish is in a "live" well filled with fresh water. Today most boats are equipped with a live well that should be large enough to store the kind of fish you are fishing for. Another very common way to temporarily store the fish is to use a fish stringer. Fish on a stringer can then be left in the same water from which they were caught, either over the side of the boat, near the shore of the stream, or next to the dock. Although many people pass the stringer through gills and mouth of the fish, the preferred method is to thread the snap-type stringer through the jaws of the fish. Thread through the upper and lower jaw for maximum security. If the stringer is passed through the gills, the fish will not live long and will begin to go soft even before it has been gutted and dressed for the grill or the frying pan. In any event, clean the fish as soon as possible to preserve the fresh taste for the table.

3. Temporary storage, as outlined above, is just that, temporary. Unless the fish is to be cooked and served right away, it should either be placed in the ice chest and/or frozen as soon as possible. If placed in the ice chest, be sure to ice the inside of the body cavity with the cracked ice. If the fish is to be frozen for longer storage, wrap the fish first with Saran wrap or any good plastic wrap to avoid freezer burn. Exposure to air is the biggest problem for the storage of any meat or fish. Even though the frozen meat or fish is still good to eat, the flavor will be gone, and the food will be tasteless. Since fish is so perishable even when it's

frozen, good plastic wrapping is the best insurance to prevent freezer burn. Another common technique for freezing smaller fish is to place the fish in water in a milk carton and freeze the entire contents.

4. If the fish is a prize catch and/or important records are to be kept, one of the first things to do is to measure the catch before it is gutted or cleaned. This is also advisable if there is a question of whether or not the fish is big enough to keep according to the current fishing laws and regulations of the state in which you are fishing. Placed on a hard, flat surface, the length, girth, and if possible, the weight of the fish should be measured at this time. If convenient scales are not available, a simple formula based on these first measurements will provide a good estimate of the weight of the fish. The formula is:

$$\text{weight of the fish in pounds} = \frac{(\text{length of fish in inches})^3}{1,600}$$

$$or \; \frac{(\text{length}) \times (\text{length}) \times (\text{length})}{1,600}$$

Another formula that is often used by a taxidermist is:

$$\text{weight in pounds} = \frac{\begin{array}{c}(\text{length of the fish in inches}) \\ \times (\text{girth of the fish in inches}) \\ \times (\text{girth of the fish in inches})\end{array}}{900 \; (\text{for fish shaped like a perch})}$$

$$\text{or } 800 \; (\text{for fish shaped like a tarpon or pike})$$

If calculators are not readily available, take the measurements of the length and girth of the fish. When these measurements are brought to the taxidermist, the weight can quickly be determined from the tabular charts in the office of the taxidermist. Be sure to measure the length of the fish from the tip of the nose to the fork in the tail. Measure the girth of the fish just behind the gill and in front of the pectoral fin. All of these measurements should be in inches, and the weight will be in pounds. The formulae and the charts referred to will be different if the measurements are metric.

5. Working with all deliberate speed, the fish should then be photographed. Color photographs are the best, and the speed of the film should, if possible, be selected according to the location, season, time of day, etc. You should remember that the color of the fish will fade rapidly once it is out of the water. This is especially true of saltwater fish. Because of the great variety of cameras, there is no attempt here to explain in detail the operation of a camera. However, for the best composition of the photograph of the fish, the following points should be observed:

   a. Try, whenever possible, to have the sun at your back. Taking a picture into the sun under any circumstances is most difficult even if you are a professional photographer. If it is a night picture, try to not have the flash closer than 3 feet from the fish and no farther away than 16 feet. This will avoid overexposure from the flash being too close to the subject and/or inadequate lighting and poor exposure from being too far away. If you're a professional photographer or very skilled in the use of the camera, you can bend these rules and still get good pictures. As an amateur, though, if you abide by these simple rules, you will get good pictures most of the time.

   b. For the best pictures, always make sure the fish is "wet." The wetness brings out the colors of the fish prominently.

   c. Have something in the picture along with the fish for a reference to the size of the fish. A rod and reel are very common props, but the fish will photograph best if held by the person who caught the fish. Most important, photograph the fish in a horizontal position. If photographed with a person, have the person hold the fish by the tail with one hand and under the gills or the head with the other. This technique of holding the fish in the horizontal position creates the common illusion that the fish is larger than it really is, or to express it another way, when held in a vertical position, the fish will seem smaller than when it is held in a horizontal position.

   d. If you have a "mess" of fish on a stringer, the common tendency is to hold the stringer vertically. Try, if possible, to hold the stringer horizontally. All of the fish will appear bigger, especially if held by a person.

e. If you are an amateur photographer and have little or no experience in operating the more sophisticated cameras, you may do an excellent job with an automatic camera, which does not require you to adjust the shutter speed, aperture, or even the focus of the lens. You simply point the camera, aim through the viewfinder, and take the picture. These cameras really save a lot of time and still get good pictures. This procedure has been further simplified by a disposable camera that is purchased with the film already contained in the camera. When all of the frames on the roll of film have been shot, all you do is turn in the entire camera with its contents to the drugstore and wait for your prints. In many cases, the wait is less than two hours. The most important thing to remember when you point and shoot with these cameras is that the fish and the person should be the main subject of the picture. That main target is what the automatic camera will focus on, and it will then make all the other necessary adjustments for the picture. The background will all be secondary, for example, the boat, the water, the sky, etc.

f. If the time and resources are available, one of the best accessories that can be added to your photographic equipment is a polarized lens. An outstanding advantage of the polarized lens is the elimination of glare on the water. This feature will many times allow pictures of subsurface subjects, such as rocks, logs, coral, and even fish, to stand out with amazing clarity.

g. Timely pictures of your fish are especially important for the taxidermist if you plan to have your fish mounted. In fact, if you are fishing for tarpon in southern Florida and are successful in landing one, you must measure it and then photograph it, since you cannot keep the fish. With a measurement of the length and girth along with a "good" photograph, the taxidermist can reproduce an almost perfect replica of the fish that is even better than if the original fish had been mounted. Using modern materials and good photographs, the mounted replica will hold its colors, shape, and configuration much better and far longer than the bones and skin of the original fish.

h.   Make sure that your camera and extra rolls of film are carried in "waterproof" containers. Since you are at and near the water (and sometimes in it), simple waterproof plastic bags are the best insurance for saving your pictures as well as your expensive equipment.

6.   Once the catch of the day has been taken from the creel or live well, measured, photographed, and placed in a portable cooler, it should be properly cleaned and dressed in preparation for cooking. Remember, if the fish is not cleaned properly, it won't taste good at the table. It is most important that before any cleaning operation is started, the proper tools and equipment should be available for the job. A cleaning table should be made available as close as possible to a running-water supply. It is best if the entire cleaning operation can be done outside.

The most important tool for cleaning fish is the filleting knife. A filleting knife with a long, flexible blade is the most preferred. The knife must be supersharp, and to keep it that way, a sharpening steel, along with a wet stone and a hone, are very helpful to have on hand. A longer blade is best for big fish, and a shorter blade can be used for smaller ones. A fish-scaling tool is needed for the smaller fish. Fish-scaling tools are very inexpensive, but in a pinch, even an old spoon will do the job. A roll of paper towels and a fish brush or a vegetable brush, along with plenty of old newspapers and disposable garbage bags, should complete the assortment of tools and equipment needed for the task.

7.   Fish under 12 inches are generally scaled and the fins removed before cooking. After the fish is gutted, hold it down on the cleaning table with the tail either clamped or held and then scrape from the tail to the head to loosen and remove the scales. Use the fish scaler, a spoon, or a dull knife. Then cut off the head behind the pectoral fins. Next, remove the fins of panfish by cutting into the flesh on both sides of each fin and pull out the fins, bones and all. Never clip the fins, since this would leave small, sharp bones in the fish. Finally, the tail may be cut off if desired.

The smaller fish, such as trout, bluegills, bream, and perch are pan-fried whole most of the time. However, if any fish is over 1 1/2 inches thick, fillet the fish first for easier cooking.

8. Generally, fish over 12 inches are either baked, poached, barbecued, smoked, cooked over an open fire, or broiled. The fish may therefore be left whole, filleted, and/or cut into steaks, if desired. In any event, be sure to cut off the "belly fat" from the steaks or fillets. This fat is not very tasty and may make the fish taste oily. Cooking fish for the table is an art form in itself. Although there are many exotic recipes that might challenge the amateur chef, there are also many simple recipes that produce delicious results. In any case, the fish must be properly field-dressed and cared for if good results are to be achieved. Poor and inadequate handling in the field can spoil even the finest catch of the day.

9. If you are fishing from a camp, a resort, or a nearby hotel, don't forget that either a guide or the chef at the hotel may prepare your catch for dinner. Check this out when you make arrangements for your fishing trip. Also, when fishing with a guide, ask if a shore lunch is included with the fishing trip. A well-prepared shore lunch in the middle of your fishing day is a memorable experience. Don't forget to ask the guide for his recipe, but first make sure the recipe is not "privileged" or the cook may charge you for this valuable information. This is especially true of the chef at the club, resort, or hotel where you have asked to have your fish cooked.

10. When your fishing is over for the day and you return home or to the fishing camp, check the fish you've caught for freshness. Even though you have just caught the fish that day, if enough time and high temperatures have prevailed, the fish can deteriorate and be spoiled for the table. Fish are very perishable, and warm weather, together with the trauma of getting caught, can make them go bad very fast. Check each fish for clear eyes, red gills, and a fresh odor. Any fish that doesn't pass this simple inspection should be rejected and definitely not cooked for the table. Incidentally, this same test should be made when buying fish at the market. Now that you have caught your fish and cleaned and dressed them for the table, you are ready for one of

the best rewards for a good day of fishing. Cooking and serving the fish for breakfast, lunch, or dinner.

11. Filleting a fish for cooking or freezing is not difficult if the filleting knife is sharp, the fish is fresh, and all of the other equipment is ready for holding the fish, catching the waste, and packaging the fillets. A sharpening steel and a honing stone are almost mandatory if the knife is to be kept sharp to cut the fillets and remove the skin, if needed. Remember to draw the cutting edge of the knife "into" the sharpening steel at a 30-degree angle as if you were trying to shave off some of the steel from the steel rod. Do about ten to fifteen strokes for each side of the cutting edge of the knife. It's important that the angle of the knife to the steel remain the same throughout each stroke of the knife to the steel. The steel is used "only" to keep the knife sharp; if you don't have a good edge on the knife to begin with, steeling will do little or no good at all. To make the knife sharp you need to sharpen it with a honing stone. Most honing stones have a course abrasive on one side and a fine-texture abrasive on the other. The best way to sharpen the knife on the honing stone is to push the blade into the stone as if you were trying to shave a thin slice off the stone. The blade should be held at a 20-degree angle to the stone continuously through each sharpening stroke. Depending on the quality of the steel, twenty to thirty strokes each way should put a fine edge on the knife.

Using a very sharp knife, the fillets can be stripped from the backbone of the fish in less than a minute. Removing the rib bones takes a little more time. If the board or table you are filleting on doesn't have a clamp or clip to hold the fish, you can use a fork or a nail to hold the head of the fish while filleting. The skin can be removed or left on. Some fish have strong-tasting skin, so it should be removed. Other fish, such as trout or panfish, have very tasty skin, which may be left on. Most importantly, if the fillets are to be cooked on the grill, leave the skin on. Once again, be sure to remove the belly fat from the fillets for a better-tasting entrée. The fish may be filleted without having been gutted, but this should only be done when the fish can be filleted very soon after the catch.

Figure 23. Filleting fish

1. Lay the fish on its side on the cleaning board, and holding the head down with the left hand, make a cut just behind the pectoral fin, behind the gill down to the backbone but not through it.

2. Start at the head with the point of the filleting knife and cut alongside the backbone toward the tail. The knife should cut down to where it starts to click along the tops of the ribs. Cut alongside the ribs, working back toward the tail until the entire side of the fish is free from the ribs and the backbone. Repeat this same procedure on the other side of the fish.

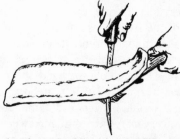

3. To remove the skin from the fillets, lay the fillet flat on the table with the skin side down. Cut loose some of the skin from the fillet near the tail. Then grasp the skin near the tail with the left hand and run the filleting knife between the skin and the fillet toward the head of the fillet, holding the blade of the knife against the inside of the skin at about a 45-degree angle. Pull on the skin with the left hand as the knife cuts with the right hand. Repeat this procedure on the other side of the fish and you will have two skinless fillets.

CHAPTER 12

The Clueless Chef Cooks the Fish

One of the most pleasant rewards of fishing is an outstanding dinner with one of the best delicacies that can be enjoyed from the stream or the sea. If you have never cooked fish before and haven't a clue as to how to start, these hints and suggestions can be helpful. There are many different recipes and techniques for cooking fish. Any method or recipe you select will depend on your taste and the particular circumstance at the time you want to cook and serve your fish. These circumstances can vary from a shore lunch with the most primitive open fire (and minimum utensils) to a formal dinner with some exotic sauces, vintage wines, and the best cooking equipment available. Following are some of the simplest procedures and recipes for the clueless chef who may have never cooked fish before. These recipes are tried-and-true, with only the minimum preparation and equipment needed to serve a delicious and even gourmet lunch or dinner.

Along with the basic cooking utensils and the basic condiments of salt, pepper, lemon juice, etc., the pantry should also include some all-purpose flour, cornbread mix, bread crumbs, vegetable cooking oil, margarine, and baking powder. Marinades are very often used in preparing fish. Marinades are seasoning used to enrich the flavor of the fish before the fish is cooked. They are also used for basting the fish while it is being cooked. After the fish is cooked, marinades are discarded most of the time. They are usually not served with the fish at the table. White wine sauce and lemon pepper are two of the most popular marinades, but in a pinch, any good salad dressing can do a good job. In any event, don't marinate the fish for more than ten minutes or it will get soggy. Any recipe and any serving of a fish entrée depend on good-quality fish to begin with. If the fish has been poorly handled from the time it was caught, the finest recipe in the world will not make it good.

Some fish caught on a fly rod will taste better if cooked on the grill or in a microwave. Others will be better if pan-fried or deep-fried. Broiling, poaching, and baking will do an excellent job on most all fish, but for fish such as salmon and trout, which are oily for the most part, broiling, poaching, grilling, and baking give the best results. Broiling and baking are the best methods for large fish, such as bass, pike, walleye, and striped bass. Smaller fish, such as panfish, small bass, and trout less than 15 inches long, do better if they are pan-fried or deep-fried. Any fish can be cooked on an open fire or simmered in chowder.

1. Open campfire cooking is one of the best and often the only convenient way to cook fish. Building the fire and controlling the heat are very important for open-fire cooking. The fire must never be too hot, for the fish can easily be overcooked. Seasoned hardwoods should also be used for the fire, since they not only burn well but can also impart a sweet flavor to the fish. Soft woods from coniferous trees, for example, pine, hemlock, and spruce, burn too fast and too hot, and they can also impart an unpleasant taste to the fish.

    If charcoal is to be used for the open campfire, make sure that the heated coals are reduced to a white ash before cooking the fish. Any remnant from the charcoal lighter fluid will impart a terrible flavor to the fish. If a gas grill is used, make sure the coals are hot enough to burn off any leftover residue from previous cooking. Fish is delicate and will pick up any foreign odors and flavors that might spoil the taste of a good dinner.

    One of the simplest ways to cook a fish over an open campfire is to first impale the whole fish, including the head and tail, on a spit. The spit can be a metal rod or strong stick of sweet hardwood. Then the fish can be roasted over an open fire. The spit or stick should run through the mouth of the fish along the backbone and out the tail. The spit or stick can be hand-held or mounted on rocks or bricks making up the fire ring and turned occasionally to thoroughly cook the fish. Keep the fire small but not too hot, with a continuous supply of dry twigs. When the meat along the backbone flakes easily with the knife or fork, the fish is done. The fish can then be skinned and boned on a plate and served, or the skin can be peeled back and the whole fish eaten like an ear of corn. Salt to taste, and with some biscuits, a vegetable, a beverage of coffee, water, or wine, a complete meal can be served.

Another popular campfire method of cooking fish is to bake or steam the fish by wrapping it in well-greased heavy aluminum foil and laying the package in the hot coals. Salt and pepper the fish, and if desired, lay two or three strips of bacon over the top of the fish. The aluminum-foil fish package should be turned once or twice and checked often so it won't be overcooked. If the fish is large, up to 4 pounds, it should be cooked about ten minutes on one side and then about ten minutes on the other. The rule of thumb is about ten minutes per inch of thickness. Measure this thickness just behind the gills. Fillets or steaks, up to 1 inch thick, should be cooked three to five minutes on one side and two to five minutes on the other side. Check frequently. When the meat parts freely from the bones, the fish is done. Don't overcook! Add wine sauce, lemon pepper, and salt to taste for a complete entrée.

2. Grilling, with the open-fire fuel supplied by charcoal, bottled gas, and sometimes just plain wood, is today one of the most popular methods of cooking fish. There are many types of grills, ranging from the simplest metal brazier with a steel grill to some very elaborate gas grills and/or barbecue pits with cast-iron grills. The smaller braziers and hibachis have the advantage of being portable, but their small size limits the amount of food that can be prepared at one time. When grilling, a hinged fish basket is very useful for small fish or even larger fish, if desired. No matter what kind of equipment you are using, though, make sure the charcoal is reduced to a white ash and that you have all of the important ancillary equipment handy for the chef to start grilling the fish. Don't ever grill inside a tent, cabin, trailer, house, or any enclosure: the carbon monoxide can kill you in minutes. Carbon monoxide is a very deadly odorless gas that is the product of the combustion of the charcoal. Grill outside, always.

Whole fish, steaks, or fillets of firm fish can be placed directly on a well-greased grill over an open fire. When cooking the fish directly on the greased grill or in a grill basket, be sure the fish and the grill are well brushed with cooking oil, such as olive oil or corn oil. Do not use melted margarine or butter on the grill; it burns up too fast, and the fish will stick to the grill. Always cook with the skin down. Cook 3–6 inches from the heat source. Grilling time for a whole fish up to 2–4 pounds will be about ten minutes on one side and ten to fifteen minutes on the other. For fillets up to 1 inch thick, the time will be about three to four minutes on one side and three to four minutes on the other. For fish steaks 1 inch thick, the time will be about five minutes on one side and three to six minutes on the other side. Check often for doneness. Use a long-handled basting brush to baste the fish frequently with oil, a marinade, or lemon-butter mix. For smaller fish or fillets, a hinged grill basket works best over the open fire. Basting with white wine, lemon pepper, and salt add a lot to the taste. In a pinch, you can always use any good salad dressing for a marinate, but don't marinate too long before you cook the fish!

3. Pan-frying fish is one of the oldest and simplest ways to cook fish. Pan-frying is quick and easy. It is most often used for smaller fish. If the fish is more than 1 1/2 inches thick, it should be filleted for easier cooking. The best frying pans are the heavy cast-iron or aluminum skillets, which distribute the heat most evenly for cooking. Cover the skillet with 1/4 inch of vegetable oil and place over medium heat; raise the temperature of the cooking oil until a drop of water sizzles when the oil is hot enough for frying. Do not cover the pan. Wipe the fish with paper towels to remove any moisture, fish slime, or loose scales. Dust the fish with flour, salt, and pepper or a coating of bread crumbs. One of the simplest bread-crumb coatings is made by dipping the fish into a mixture of milk and one beaten egg. Then dredge the fish in the flour, cornmeal, bread crumbs, or cornflake crumbs. You may now fry over a medium heat for three to five minutes, then two to five minutes on the second side. Test for doneness with a fork at the backbone and twist. When done, the meat will separate easily from the bones. Whole fish up to 1 1/2 inches thick will cook in three to five minutes on one side and from two to five minutes on the other. Thin fillets (1/4 inch) will cook in three minutes on the

first side and up to two minutes on the second side. Thick fillets (1 inch) may take up to five minutes on the first side and three to four minutes on the second side.

4. Deep-frying is another method of preparation that provides a very tasty entrée of fish fillets for larger numbers of patrons of the surf, lake, or stream. The most traditional method of deep-frying requires a deep-fryer pan or a tall saucepan with 3 or 4 inches of cooking oil in the bottom of the pan. The advantage of the high sides of the pan is the ability to catch the splatters of hot oil while cooking the fish. You can also use a large skillet with half as much oil in the bottom, but extra care must be taken to control the splatter. The temperature of the cooking oil has to be raised to about 375 degrees Fahrenheit and should be checked each time a new batch of fish is added to the oil. If the fish and batter are cold and the oil is up to temperature, the cooked fish will be moist and flaky inside and crispy golden brown on the outside. Cooking times for fillets from 1/4 to 1 inch thick will be from three to five minutes. Try a small fillet first and taste to make sure cooking temperature and time are correct. The fish fillets should first be chilled in the refrigerator and then patted dry on paper towels. The fish should then be dipped in the batter and then gently dropped into the hot oil, one fillet at a time. When the battered fish is golden brown, the fish is done. Drain the fish on some paper towels and serve.

There are many batters, including the ones described for pan-frying as well as those commercially packaged. A box of prepackaged batter mix is a good addition to the food supplies when on a fishing trip. One of the most famous batters for deep-frying is the beer batter. This recipe can use any beer.

Beer Batter

1 cup all-purpose flour	1 cup beer
3 tablespoons cornstarch	1 tablespoon vegetable oil
1/2 teaspoon paprika and/or dash nutmeg	

Mix the dry ingredients and blend in the beer and vegetable oil until smooth. Dip the fish into the batter and deep-fry as indicated. These ingredients will make about 1 1/2 cups of batter.

5. Broiling is one of the most palatable ways to prepare fish for the table. The most significant difference between broiling and other cooking methods is that the cooking heat will come from the top down to the fish on the rack, which is resting on the broiler pan. Fillets should always be placed on the rack, skin side down. Whole fish, especially if they are large, should be turned about halfway through the broiling time. Any fish can be broiled, but care must be used to preserve the moisture because of the high heat from the broiler fire. About 3–4 inches from the fire is best for most broilers. Constant basting with oil or lemon butter will keep the fish from drying out most of the time.

   Many commercial chefs in good restaurants will employ a technique not too well known to the public. First the fish or the fillet (up to 1 inch) is "baked" in a 350-degree oven for four or five minutes. Then the fish (or fillet) is brushed with the lemon butter and broiled for three to five minutes. This will produce a fillet or whole fish that is done to perfection. Total cooking time for this entrée will then be about eight to ten minutes. If the whole fish, the fillets, or the steaks are more or less than 1 inch, these times will have to be adjusted.

6. Poaching will enhance the flavor of almost any fish. The technique is so simple that it is surprising that it is not used more often than it is. In the kitchen or at the campfire, use the same heavy skillet that was used to pan-fry fish. Instead of cooking oil, use some margarine to cover the bottom of the pan and then add about a 1/2 inch of milk. Heat until the milk starts to steam but does not boil. Add the salted fish and cover the pan. Simmer for about ten minutes. Remove from the fire, drain, and serve. A vegetable broth or bouillon with a little white wine may be substituted for the milk if desired.

   A whole fish, or just the fish steaks and/or fillets, may be poached this way. The procedure is the same. If a whole fish is used, leave the head on if possible. If the fish is too big, cut off the head and set it in the poaching liquid. The head adds more flavor to the rest of the fish. Test for doneness by inserting a fork between the dorsal fin and the head. The fish is done when it flakes away from the bone and skin easily. There are many other recipes for the poaching liquid, but the cooking procedure is the same.

Poaching is one of the easiest ways to cook fish over an open campfire or on the stove in the kitchen. With the freshly caught fish that has been properly gutted, prepare 1/4 cup of vinegar with just enough water to cover the fish in a skillet. Do not wipe the slime off the fish. This will add some color and taste to the fish. Bring the vinegar water to a boil, turn down the heat, and place the whole fish into the laughing water. Poach (simmer) for six minutes. A very tasty change of pace for the camp diet. A good variation for this recipe is to use white wine instead of vinegar for the poaching liquid.

7. Steaming follows the same procedure as poaching except that instead of the fish being immersed in the liquid, it is placed on a rack, which holds the fish just above the boiling liquid. The liquid is usually a bouillon or water and white wine. Cooking time for steaming or poaching is not as critical as it is for other procedures. Fish cooked a couple of minutes longer will not be overdone. The same rule applies for cooking times, about ten minutes per inch of thickness for whole fish or fillets and steaks. Shorten the time for fillets under 1 inch.

8. Fish chowder can be made for a complete meal or just a light appetizer. The soup can be made from fresh fish or cooked left-overs. After adding the fish, you have to watch the chowder, since the fish can easily be overcooked. Refrigerate leftover soup and use within two days. If frozen in containers, the soup should be used within a month. One of the simplest chowders can be made over the open campfire by cutting the fish fillets into 1-inch-square pieces and laid on top of chopped bacon strips, diced onions, and about six diced potatoes. The bacon is first simmered in the pot before the other ingredients are added. The pot is then filled with water up to the top of the fish. Salt and pepper are added to taste. After the pot has been brought to a boil, add some oregano leaves, a little sage, and a bay leaf. Let it simmer for about an hour. Then add a half-stick of margarine and two cups of milk. Stir slowly and serve.

9. Baking is one of the oldest and most traditional ways to cook fish. It is ideal for a large whole fish as well as fillets and steaks. There are many recipes for stuffing a whole fish as well as sauces for fillets and steaks. Oven temperature for baking is about 375

degrees Fahrenheit. Cooking times are ten minutes plus ten minutes per pound. The fish must be watched carefully so it doesn't dry out. Some baking recipes require more ingredients than others do. Whole fish or fillets may be baked in heavy aluminum foil with nothing more than some butter and parsley added for moisture and taste, or more elaborate recipes may be used.

One of the simplest recipes for the clueless chef to follow is for parmesan fish bake.

Parmesan Fish Bake

4 fish fillets (about 2 pounds)	2 tablespoons parsley flakes
1 stick melted butter	1/2 teaspoon salt
1/2 cup grated Parmesan cheese	1/4 teaspoon pepper
1 1/4 cup soda cracker crumbs	1/2 lemon

Dip the fish into the melted butter. Combine the Parmesan cheese, cracker crumbs, and seasonings and roll the buttered fish in the mixture. Place in a shallow 9-by-13 inch baking dish. Place the remaining crumbs and butter over the top of the fish. Bake uncovered in a 375-degree oven for about twenty-five minutes or until the fish flakes. Squeeze the lemon over the fish and serve. This recipe should serve about four people.

Another tasty recipe for baking fillets or steaks is fish au gratin.

Fish Au Gratin

1 cup chicken or vegetable broth
1 tablespoon all-purpose flour
1 tablespoon margarine or butter
1 teaspoon salt
1/4 teaspoon pepper
pinch of ground thyme
1/4 cup whipping cream or heavy cream
1 1/2 pounds boneless fillets of lake trout, red snapper, walleye pike, scrod, or salmon
3 tablespoons grated Parmesan, Swiss, or Guyere cheese
2 tablespoons dry bread crumbs
1 tablespoon melted margarine or butter
1 teaspoon lemon juice

Bring the broth to a boiling point in a small saucepan. Blend the flour into the butter and stir into the boiling broth. Cook and stir until thickened. Reduce the heat and stir in salt, pepper, thyme, and cream. Place the fish in a well-buttered baking pan. Pour the sauce over the fish. Bake at 375 degrees Fahrenheit for fifteen minutes. Mix the cheese, bread crumbs, melted butter, and lemon juice. Sprinkle over the fish and bake fifteen minutes longer or until the fish flakes easily. This recipe serves four to six people.

10. Microwaving is one of the fastest ways to cook fish with a minimum amount of equipment and preparation. The speed and moisture retention of microwaving are decided advantages, but constant attention and care must be taken to avoid overcooking the fish. It is very easy to overcook the fish with a microwave; doing so will dry out and toughen the fish. There is also a substantial variation in the cooking power generated by the many different microwaves as well as different methods of rotating the food in the microwave. These variations mean that each cooking procedure must be adjusted to fit the individual microwave that is being used. Generally speaking, the recipes for baking, poaching, and steaming that have been outlined here can be followed with the obvious change that all baking pans, etc., must be made of materials compatible with the microwave. No metal is allowed. Cooking times will vary from eight to ten minutes at 50 percent power for small whole fish; from three to five minutes at full power; and from five to ten minutes at full power for thick steaks. All of these suggestions are for a fish that is not frozen. If for any reason the fish has been frozen, it should be first thoroughly thawed before attempting to cook in the microwave. In addition, when poaching or steaming in the microwave, cover the fish loosely with wax paper to avoid splattering the inside of the microwave.

A note to the clueless chef: Please remember that all of these units of measurement, a pinch, a teaspoon, etc., are based on American units of measurement. Any such measurements in metric, England, or the United Kingdom will be different.

Whenever fish is being served, whether for a gourmet dinner or for a shore lunch at the fishing camp, certain other foods and beverages can enhance and complement this delightful entrée. It is most important that there should always be bread on the table along with the fish entrée. No matter how much care is taken, there is always the possibility of a fish bone being served with the fish. If a fish bone is caught in one's throat, it can be very harmful. Bread can be very helpful, along with the Heimlich maneuver, to dislodge a sharp fish bone.

Condiments for fish are very popular. One of the most common, tartar sauce, can be obtained in small 8-ounce jars at the supermarket and carried to the fishing camp. A simple mix of mayonnaise (1 cup), minced parsley (2 tablespoons), some minced onion (2 tablespoons), and minced dill pickle (3 tablespoons), along with 2 tablespoons of fresh lime or lemon juice, will make about 1 1/4 cups of the sauce for the kitchen at home. Two tablespoons of minced pimento-stuffed olives will add a lot to the flavor. Another condiment that will add a more exotic touch to the fish and will be easy to prepare at home or in the camp is strawberry jam mixed with horseradish. Mix the amount of horseradish to suit your own taste. Be careful; too much can overwhelm the fish. Another condiment is a mixture of cream of coconut and crushed pineapple mixed to suite your taste.

One of the oldest and most popular beverages to be served with fish is wine. Many people, especially those who haven't fished before, haven't a clue as to the best wine to serve with their catch of the day. Certain guidelines can be helpful in selecting a good wine for the occasion. Final judgments, of course, will depend on each individual's taste, but for the clueless these points can be helpful. There are five basic categories of wines. These are the appetizer wines, the white table wines, the red table wines, sweet dessert wines, and the sparkling wines. Traditionally, white wines are served with white meats such as fish, seafood, and poultry. Red wines are generally served with the red meats, and sparkling wines are served with any food. Sweet dessert wines are served with desserts or at any time for in-between meal refreshments.

Ampelographers (wine experts) tell us that all white wines should be served chilled at about 55 degrees Fahrenheit and that red wines should be served at about room temperature or just slightly chilled. Sparkling wines, usually served for special occasions, are always served chilled. Champagne, of course, should always be served at 37–45 degrees Fahrenheit. Also note that all wines, even including the jug wines, should be stored at 55 degrees Fahrenheit, with the bottles laid on their sides to keep the corks wet. If they are stored in the vertical position and exposed to sunlight, the wine will turn to vinegar.

Some of the more popular white wines that will serve well with fish are as follows:

Blanc de Blancs	White wine made from white grapes
Chablis	Dry, fruity pale gold wine made from several different grapes
Chardonnay	Dry varietal wine with distinctive flavor and aroma of Chardonnay grapes
Chenis Blanc	Dry to semisweet, light-bodied, fragrant Chablis-type wine
Pinot Blanc	Dry, tart Chablis-type wine made from Pinot Blanc grapes
Riesling	Rhine wine made from one or a blend of Riesling grapes
Sauvignon Blanc	Sauterne-type wine, flavor and aroma of Sauvignon Blanc grapes, usually dry

As noted in so many of the recipes for cooking fish, wine adds and enhances the flavor so much that it's almost a gross omission not to use it when called for in the recipe. If the alcohol content gives you a problem, don't worry about it. The alcohol content of the wine quickly evaporates; all that remains is the flavor. Also remember that jug wines (the most inexpensive) are great for cooking; you don't need an expensive vintage to cook with. Remember that when the champagne has lost its bubble, the wine remaining is great for poaching fish. If you add some celery stalks and leaves, a slice of onion, peppercorns, and a pinch of thyme, you will have a delicious sauce for the fish. Just remember to cork it tightly when you store it in the refrigerator. When you are in a hurry, though, about the most simple sauce you can make for broiling or barbecuing your fish is to mix equal parts of melted butter and dry white wine with a dash of herbs for basting the fillets or fish steaks. Wine has so many applications for cooking that it's a shame not to use it for your fish dishes.

CHAPTER 13

Laws, Ethics, Good Manners, and Safety for Good Fishing

Yes, there is a legal requirement that must be satisfied before you can start fishing. As far as we know, every one of the fifty states requires a license. In most states children under sixteen, members of the armed forces, and in some cases, senior citizens are exempt from these laws; but for everyone else a license is required. In many states the spouse of a license holder is also exempt, but this is not true everywhere. Check with any local bait store, sporting-goods store, or the State Department of Fisheries to be sure of what the requirements are in your state. Along with the license application form issued by the Fisheries Division of your State Natural Resources or Conservation Department, all states publish a fishing guide that outlines all of the rules and regulations for fishing the waters of your state. These guides are free, and they are usually available wherever fishing licenses are sold. The guides make very clear what the license requirements are, how big the fish must be, how many fish you may take, and how many you may possess each day or for the season. In addition, these guides usually include a wealth of other important information, for example, the fishing seasons for each of the fish species, special waters reserved for fly-fishing only, or holy waters for catch and release only. Once you have started fly-fishing, keep one of these guides handy whenever you go fishing.

Don't forget the Internet, where most of this information is readily available twenty-four hours a day. In addition, if you are going to fish in a state other than your own, make sure you know the requirements for that state. Fishing-license requirements differ from state to state. Saltwater license requirements are often different from freshwater license requirements; in many cases, a separate license is needed along with the freshwater license. When fishing for trout or salmon, a separate "trout" stamp is often required along with the regular fishing license. On the lighter side, however, it should be pointed out that most states offer a temporary one-day, three-day, or even seven-day license for the visitor from another state who wants to fish on his or her vacation. It's important to know that a "license" is permission to fish and take the state's property. All fish and wild game are property of the state until they are legally reduced to the possession of the hunter or fisher person.

The license for the angler to take these fish is a privilege from the state, not a contract or a property right; a license is a mere personal permit. This is very important, since the state must not only regulate the fisheries and the habitat; they must also maintain the fisheries for disease control, restocking, and stream and lake access for the angler. In support of these important functions there is a great deal of research and field inspections that go on every day. Practically all of these operations are funded from the sale of fishing licenses. Although some people take umbrage at these rules and regulations and the people who have to enforce them, we should always remember that without them, there would be no sport fishing at all!

The administrators, biologists, ichthyologists, engineers, and enforcement officers are very good at what they do, working just so you can fish and enjoy the outdoors. Incidentally, these people, in most cases, are also a walking encyclopedia of information on fish locations, insect hatches, and most fishing conditions. If you don't meet them in the woods or on the water, don't hesitate to telephone them. The enforcement officers (also called game wardens or conservation officers) who patrol the lakes, streams, and forest are always properly uniformed and very polite, so there is no mistake about who they are or what their business is. That business not only includes fishing conditions but forest-fire prevention, water-pollution surveillance, and public safety. They're always ready to help you with valuable information. If you are ever requested to show your fishing license or the fish you may have in your possession, don't ever say to an enforcement officer that you haven't a clue as to what the legal requirements are for you to fish. Remember that ignorance of the law is no excuse. The rules and regulations not only say who must have a license, but they also prescribe

the number of fish you may have in your possession and the size of
the fish that you may keep. In certain waters often referred to as
holy waters (catch-and-release waters), the rules may even prevent
you from keeping any of the fish. More and more catch-and-release
waters are being designated every day. Another fairly common reg-
ulation for many designated streams and lakes requires flies only
for any type of fishing. Wherever you are going to fish, check the
rules and regulations first to save frustration and disappointment
on your fishing trip. The enforcement officers can be very unforgiving of such infractions, and the penalties are not light. In many
cases, all of the fishing tackle, and in some cases even the automobile and/or boat, can be impounded. Then there will be a hearing
before a magistrate, and he or she will make a judgment call for the
penalty. This can be awkward and embarrassing, and very expensive as well.

Some other important legal issues that anglers are often confronted with are the questions of public property, private property,
and trespass. When fishing on steams, lakes, and in national or
state parks in our state and national forests, these questions will almost always be moot, but there is a tremendous amount of private
land adjoining these public lands and waters that can be a problem
for the angler if the legal issue of trespass is not understood. Trespass is the unlawful interference with one's person, property, or
rights. In most cases, the private property adjoining fishing waters
will be posted identifying the land as private property, and in many
cases the land will also be fenced. Encroaching on these private
properties without permission is trespassing. Unlike the failure to
possess a fishing license, which is a misdemeanor against the state,
trespassing is a personal wrong, or a tort, which will be grounds for
a civil action against the violator to satisfy the injury. What this
also means is that as long as you stay in the water or on the bed of
the stream, you are not trespassing on private property.

A most important fact to know is that practically all of the
water in our rivers, streams, and lakes is public and belongs to the
state. The bed of the stream or lake is also public, and the angler
who is wading or in his canoe or MacKenzie drift boat is entitled
to complete use of these waters. The one qualification for these
provisions is that the waterway, stream, etc., must be "navigable."
The general rule for the definition of a navigable stream or body of

water is that a log must be able to be floated downstream and/or across the water. This definition is used to distinguish the waterway from an intermittent drainage ditch. A problem can arise if and when the angler leaves the stream or lake and enters onto the shoreline without the permission of the landowner. If this property is private property, such an unauthorized entry could well be a trespass. Remember that a fishing license is not a license to trespass on private property without the owner's permission. If you are wading in a stream, paddling your canoe, or driving your motorboat, check for fences and/or posting on the shoreline before you step ashore.

ETHICS

Ethics for the angler fly-fishing on lake, stream, or ocean include certain standards of personal conduct. These standards are essentially no more than good manners necessary to maintain good relationships with other anglers, and they can even be self-serving for better fishing. Some, but not all, of these standards are:

1. Any pool or reasonably definable stretch of water belongs to the first person fishing it.
2. Allow at least 200 feet before fishing ahead of another angler. This means 200 feet beyond the reach of your fly line. In other words, don't cast into another angler's fishing water.
3. Leave the water and walk around a slow-moving angler. Never walk along a bank a person is casting toward.
4. Be careful not to cast your silhouette over a pool that someone else is fishing.
5. Don't watch a person fishing a pool or stretch of water without asking if it interferes with their fishing.
6. Never get into a pool or stretch of water that is already being fished without asking the other angler's permission.
7. Never enter a stream too close to another angler.
8. Too much noise when wading or in a boat is always poor manners.
9. Traditionally, the angler wading upstream has the right of way over the angler wading downstream.
10. Respect private property.

11. Clean up the site after you have used the water and the shore for your fishing. The shore lunch is a common and most enjoyable part of the fishing day, but when you are finished, clean up and make sure all fires are completely out.

SAFETY

Safety for the angler is paramount anytime or anywhere when fishing. Nothing can spoil a fishing trip more than a mishap that could have been avoided and/or was not addressed right away. A properly stocked first-aid kit is, of course, standard equipment for any fishing trip or outing. While actually fishing, there are three types of accidents that are the most common for anglers. First, and perhaps most dangerous, is falling. Second, and perhaps most common, is hooking yourself or another person. Third, and perhaps most painful, is being bitten or cut on the hands by a fish. Along with these unforeseen accidents, we must include some of the most frequent problems encountered by anyone in the outdoors. By far one of the worst and most common problems is sunburn. On or near the water, the exposure to the harmful rays of the sun can be amplified to a most unpleasant degree. Don't believe that you're immune or protected simply because you are wearing a hat with a wide brim. The reflection of the sun from the water is almost as intense as the sun itself, and the burns can afflict you in places you would never expect, for example, under your chin or nose, your ears, and even your hands. Be prepared; use sunscreen. When in doubt, use more sunscreen. Don't take risks that can spoil your fishing trip.

Other common problems for the clueless angler who hasn't spent much time fishing, although not life threatening, would be poison ivy and/or poison oak and bites from wild animals. Some of the more annoying problems in the outdoors are bites from the undesirable members of the insect world, such as mosquitoes, bees, wasps, deerflies, and no-see-ums. Be especially careful if you are allergic to the stings of bees and/or deerflies; these bites can be life threatening to those who forget to carry their medicine kits with them. Even if you are not allergic, you will be eternally grateful if you carry some insect repellent in your fishing vest or your tackle box. In the summertime, after a walk in the woods, check your clothes and boots for deer ticks. In eastern North America this small tick (about 1/8 inch) feeds on mammals, especially deer, and can easily be picked up on your clothing from the weeds and plants in the woods. A bite from these ticks can transmit Lyme disease, which can be painful and debilitating. Most important for the clueless angler, do not use perfume, after-shave lotion, scented deodorant, or even scented soap just before you start fishing. Nothing attracts mosquitoes, flies, and even no-see-ums more than the sweet scent of these personal additions to your daily bath or shower in spite of the insect repellent you may have applied. Remember, under the right atmospheric conditions, these scents can be detected from as far away as 100 feet from the source. Protect yourself; don't smell so sweet. Even lipstick and powder will attract these undesirable visitors.

Falls that occur when you are wading in fast-flowing streams with irregular bottoms or slippery rocks happen most of the time in shallow water. It's easy to lose your balance, especially if you are not familiar with the stream and you don't have a wading staff. In deeper water you tend to be more cautious, and the water pressure from the deep water helps keep your balance. The best way to avoid falls is to make sure you have a wading staff and wear the proper wading boot or shoe that has a heel and sole that can best grip the type of bottom where you are wading. Chest waders are most often preferred for wading the lakes, rivers, and streams. Hippers have their place, too, but the chest waders are preferred for most fishing situations. Rubber-cleat soles are best for sand, gravel, soft silt, or mud. Felt soles are best for bottoms made up of large boulders, big stones, or flat pieces of broken bedrock, which are often covered with slick algae. In any event, be very careful when walking on slippery banks of wet mud, clay, or ground covered with leaves. Some boot soles have felt or soft metal stud or cleat combinations that are used in swift water with slippery rock bottoms.

Good boots are a tremendous asset when wading, but they will not make up for improper or careless footwork when you are in a stream or a saltwater tidal flat. Wade carefully! Use a wading staff and make sure your belt is tightened on your waders. Move step by step. Don't pick up one foot until the other one is firmly placed down. Move slowly; it's not only safer, but it doesn't spook the fish and is more conducive to better fishing. Use polarized glasses and watch for underwater logs, drop-offs, submerged boulders, and other pitfalls.

If you do fall down and the water is over your head, hold on to your fly rod. You won't hurt the rod, and you can use it the same way an acrobat uses a rod for balance when on a tightrope. Don't fight the current and try to relax. Go with the current with your feet downstream and your head upstream until you reach shallower water and a bush or tree by the riverbank to help you ashore. An excellent exercise in good water safety is to submerge yourself in a swimming pool or a lake with your waders on. When you try this experiment, have a friend standing by for help. This will give you a good feel for the conditions you can expect if you ever have an accident in the stream and may well save your life or the life of one of your companions. If you are handicapped or very uncertain about the water in which you will be wading, give serious consideration to a fishing vest with a built-in life preserver. This is a regular fishing vest with a carbon dioxide cartridge that will inflate the vest as soon as the chord is pulled. The inflated vest will keep your head above the water until you can regain your footing in the water.

Bites from Fish

Bites from fish or punctures from their fins can be very painful and even dangerous if they become infected. Use common sense and some simple precautions to avoid these unnecessary mishaps. Although all fish don't have sharp teeth, many of them do, so play it safe and keep your hands out of their mouths. It's also true that all fish don't have fins with spines, but many of them do, so again, play it safe and keep your hands away from the fins of the fish. This is also true about the gill plates, so avoid these as well and be safe rather than sorry. In general, be very careful when landing your fish. Use a landing net or beach it when possible. If you use a hemostat, needle-nose pliers, or a hook disgorge to remove hooks from the fish, you should avoid these problems practically all of the time.

Hooking Accidents

Hooking accidents even happen to professionals if they spend enough time fishing. Most of these accidents, if handled properly, amount to no more than an inconvenient nuisance. Most dangerous are those accidents where the hook is embedded near the eyes or in the throat. In these cases, emergency treatment at a hospital is required as soon as possible. All other wounds from a hook can be handled with some simple procedures. The most important rule for any of these mishaps is to avoid panic. Because of the limited size of these hooks, none of these wounds is life-threatening, and the amount of tissue damage is very small. With the exception of the eye and throat wounds, all hooks can be removed quickly without pain (see Fig. 24). Although you can do these procedures yourself, it is less painful and more efficient, in most cases, if your companion or someone else can do it for you.

The first procedure is to cut off the leader from the hook at or very near the fly. Set the fly rod aside. Examine the wound to see if the barb of the hook is buried or has turned and exited the skin. If the barb is buried past the bend, press the eye of the hook down against the skin with your finger. Then, with a long-nose pliers or a piece of monofilament passed through the opening between the skin and the bend of the hook, make a quick, firm pull on the pliers or monofilament away from the direction that the hook entered. The hook should pop out immediately with little pain and little damage to the skin. If there is some blood, so much the better. Let the wound bleed a little to flush out any foreign material and then cover with a Band-Aid. If bleeding continues, apply some pressure and add more tape to the bandage. Some iodine or antibiotic cream would also be helpful.

If the hook has turned so that the point and barb are exposed next to the wound where it entered the skin, then the hook point and barb should be cut off from the bend of the hook with a pair of wire cutters. Long-nose pliers usually have wire cutters at the base of the long-nose grips. If wire cutters are not available, don't attempt to remove the hook. Go to a clinic or hospital where a physician can remove it safely. If the barb of the hook hasn't cleared the skin, push the shank of the hook so that the barb is exposed. Then proceed with the wire cutters to cut off the barb and point of the hook. Once this is done, the hook can be backed out from the wound with little difficulty. Once again, a little bleeding will help flush out the wound. Then apply some antiseptic and cover the wound with a bandage. In any case, check with a physician as soon as convenient to see if a tetanus shot is needed.

Figure 24. Removing a hook that has penetrated the skin beyond the barb

1. Cut the leader.

2. Press down with the thumb on the eye of the hook against the skin.

3. Press down on the eye of the hook against the skin and pull the bend of the hook with the long-nose pliers until the point and barb of the hook are free from the skin.

How to remove a hook when the point has penetrated the skin and then emerged, exposing the point and the barb.

1.   Cut the leader.

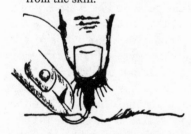 

2. Cut off the point and the barb of the hook just above where it emerged from the skin.

3. Back out the bend of the hook (without the point and barb) from the penetration.

Most hooking accidents occur when the angler makes a back-cast and doesn't see the other person or when a fly gets caught in a bush or tree and the angler snaps the rod in an attempt to free the line. When the fly snaps free, it can fly through the air like an arrow and may well hit the angler in the face. Only careful removal of the fly from the tree can avoid this unhappy experience. Many times it is just better to cut the tippet and forfeit the fly.

FLY-FISHING GLOSSARY

Action   The manner in which a fly rod operates. A measurement of flexibility and power.

AFTMA   The American Fishing Tackle Manufacturing Association. Manufacturers organized to maintain standards for the production of fishing tackle.

Ambient temperature   The temperature of the atmosphere, water, or other substance that surrounds the entire group of people, fish in the river, the forest, etc.

Anadromous   Fish that move up the streams and rivers from the oceans and large lakes for the purpose of spawning (breeding).

Arbor   The spindle of a fly-fishing reel to which the backing line and fly line are attached.

Aquatic insects   A substantial group of invertebrate animals known as "insects" of the phylum Arthropoda. There are many different species of insects. Those insects that live most of their normal life cycle underwater are known as aquatic insects.

Attracter   A very bright color in a fishing lure or fly.

Backing   A fishing line of either nylon or Dacron mounted on the arbor of a reel. It is used to support and extend the use of a conventional fly line. It may be several hundred feet in length and comes into play when landing big fish.

Backlash   A snarl of fishing line wound on a reel.

Bank   The steep earth or rock sides of a river or lake above the waterline.

Bar   Any kind of structure in a stream, lake, or tidal basin that interferes with the flow of the water, for example, logs, sandbars, stumps, grass, etc.

Barb   A raised, pointed part of a hook just behind the main point of the hook that prevents the hook from coming out of the fish's mouth.

Barbless hook   A hook without a barb. Used in fly-fishing for catch-and-release fishing.

Bass   A term used for a large group of freshwater sunfish such as largemouth bass, smallmouth bass, or even rock bass.

Bass bug   A floating fly or popper used for fly-fishing for bass.

Beaching   A technique of landing a fish that has been hooked by moving it to the beach of the lake or river.

Beaver pond   A small lake or pond that has been formed by beavers building a dam on a stream or river.

Belly   The curve of a fly line floating on the water formed by the current and/or the wind. It is also the midsection of a fly line.

Bite   The strike or hit of a fish on a bait, lure, or artificial fly. The bite is also the distance from the point of a hook to the extent of the bend of the hook.

Billfish   General term referring to the family of fishes Istiophoridae, which includes the swordfish and other spearfish, such as sailfish and marlins. Also called big-game fish.

Brackish   Fresh water, usually from a freshwater stream or river, mixed with salt water from the ocean. Brackish water usually occurs in coastal estuaries and bays.

Bucktail   A wet streamer fly made up of deer hair and feathers.

Bug   A term usually applied to any insect that creeps, flies, or crawls, but more frequently applied to an artificial fly that imitates large insects, frogs, etc., used to fish for panfish, bass, and sometimes trout.

Butt cap   The end of a fly-rod handle used to protect the end of the fly rod.

Canal   A man-made ditch filled with water made to connect lakes, ponds, or swamps to equalize the flow of water between the lakes or to provide transportation for boats, barges, etc.

Cast   The procedure for throwing a fly line, leader, tippet, and fly onto the water with a fly rod.

Catadromous   Fish that live in fresh water and move out to sea to spawn.

Catch and release   Catching fish and then releasing them alive and unharmed.

Caudal fin   The tail fin of a fish. This fin is used primarily for locomotion, especially for a sudden burst of speed.

Channel   A relatively deep part of a river or stream usually made by either man-made excavations or the current of the river.

Char   A large group of popular freshwater fish that includes brook trout, lake trout, arctic char, and Dolly Varden.

Chenille   A fly-tying thread or fluffy material made up of rayon, wool, or nylon used to make wet artificial flies such as the wooly worm.

Chumline   Cut-up pieces of fish food put into the water to attract hungry fish to a specific area near the angler.

Clippers   A small tool used to cut and trim the fly line, leader, or tippet.

Cold-water fish   Fish that thrive in water temperatures ranging from 40–65 degrees Fahrenheit, for example, trout and salmon.

Cool water   Fish that do best in water temperatures ranging from 55–75 degrees Fahrenheit, for example, bass, walleyes, or northern pike.

Cove   A small indentation of the shoreline of a river, tidal flat, or lake.

Crayfish   A small crustacean that looks like a small lobster. Very popular as fish food.

Creel   A bag, basket, or other container carried by anglers to keep fish (the catch of the day). The creel is usually kept cool by being suspended in water.

Cruising   Fish moving about in a lake or stream searching for food.

Current   The movement of water in a stream, river, and sometimes in a lake or ocean, with a definite velocity. Sometimes this velocity is strong enough to move sand, gravel, stones, logs, and even people downstream from where they entered the lake or stream. Most often the current brings food to the fish.

Crepuscular   The description of an insect or fish that is more active at twilight or nighttime.

Dead drift   The drift of a fly or popper downstream or out into the lake caused by the current, tide, or wind. It also means that there is no drag on the fly from the leader.

Dead head   A submerged log or other debris very often floating in the water that can hit a boat or snag a fly. Usually a hazard.

Deer hair   Hair from a deer hide used for tying many different fly designs.

Density   This term is most often used in fly-fishing to describe the relative weight of such items as the fly line, leaders, and sometimes even the fly when used in relation to the water.

Dorsal fin   A relatively large, spiny fin on the upper backbone of a fish.

DNR   The Department of Natural Resources. Most often the branch of state government that regulates the fisheries of the state.

Double hook   A fly hook that has essentially two hooks with one common shank. It is very often used for making salmon flies.

Drag   The force from the wind or the current that causes the fly line to pull unnaturally on the fly on or through the water.

Dress   The application of waterproofing material to the fly line or the fly.

Drift   The movement of a fly on the water while it is fished on the stream's current.

Dry fly   An artificial fly design that allows the fly to float on the surface of the water.

Dropper   Additional fly tied to the leader ahead of the point fly. Usually a dry fly.

Dubbing A fly-tying material made up of natural hairs and synthetic fibers blended into a wrapping used to form the body of many dry and wet flies.

Dun The first adult stage of an aquatic mayfly insect. This is also called a subimago, and it is one of the last stages of the insect's life cycle. The wings have just formed, and the insect is resting on the water waiting for the wings to dry out so it can rise for the mating stage of its life.

Ebb tide The tide (salt water) while ebbing or moving out.

Eddy A slow-swirling water disturbance in the flow of a river or stream caused by an obstruction such as a submerged log or boulder.

Emerger A stage of the life cycle of an aquatic insect when it swims to the surface of the water to hatch or emerge from the nymph stage to the full-adult or dun stage.

Entomology That branch of zoology that deals with insects. Since insects make up so much of the food supply for fish, entomology is very important to fishing, especially fly-fishing.

Epidemiologist A specialist in that branch of science that deals with the incidence, distribution, and control of disease. Especially important today in dealing with whirling disease of rainbow trout, pollution of lakes, etc.

Feeding The period or time of day or night when fish feed.

Fighting The struggle to land a fish after the fish has been hooked.

Fingerling A small fish about finger length in size, most often used to describe small, immature bass, trout, or any other game fish.

Fishing vest A lightweight vest with many assorted pockets for carrying various flies, hooks, thermometers, clippers, candy bars, sunscreen, and many other essentials for fly-fishing.

Fish on A signal announced to everyone else in the boat or nearby on the stream that a fish has been hooked and is being played to be landed in the net. The other anglers will then reel in their lines and stand clear so as not to interfere with the landing of the fish.

Flat   A relatively wide section of smooth water surface on a stream, lake, or tidal flat.

Flex   That property of a fly rod that indicates the amount of bending of the rod when casting a fly on a fly line. A stiff rod will flex primarily from the tip of the rod. A medium-flex rod will bend mostly from the center of the rod. A soft rod will flex almost from the handle.

Flood tide   The flowing in of the tide (salt water). A rising tide.

Fly   A combination of fur, feathers, yarn, and a hook assembled to imitate the size, shape, and sometimes the color of a natural nymph or mature insect.

Fresh water   Rivers, streams, ponds, or lakes that have very little or no salt in the water. The term is also used to describe fish that live only in a habitat of fresh water.

Fry   The first stage of development of a fish after hatching from an egg or live birth. Usually from 1/2–2 inches in length.

Gaff   A fairly large sharp-pointed hook mounted on a pole used to hook and capture a large fish that has been brought close to the boat by the angler. The term is also used as a verb to describe the act of capturing a fish once it has been brought to the boat with rod and reel.

Game fish   Those fish usually designated by sportsmen and some state fisheries as especially challenging for the angler to catch (and sometimes release).

Gap   The distance between the hook shank and the hook point.

Gill   The respiratory organ of a fish located just behind the head.

Grilse   A small salmon, 3–8 pounds.

Grain   The unit of measurement used for measuring the weight of a fly line. There are 437.5 grains to the ounce, or 7,000 grains to the pound.

Hackle   Feathers from the neck and/or back of a chicken, grouse, or turkey.

Handle   That part of a fly rod, usually made of cork, used for holding the rod while casting or landing a fish.

Hauling   A technique for increasing fly-line speed during pick-up, backcasting, or forward casting. It is performed by pulling by hand on the fly line (stripping) between the reel and stripper guide of the rod.

High-water slack   The high-water period between the flood tide (high) and the ebb tide (outgoing) when the water is not moving.

Hold   A place where fish such as trout, bass, or salmon will remain stationary while they feed or just rest.

Hook   A bent piece of wire with a sharp point and barb at one end used to catch and hold a fish that strikes or attempts to eat the imitation fly or lure surrounding the hook.

Hook barb   The raised metal point off the hook's main point. The barb prevents the hook from backing out of the jaw of the fish.

Hook bend   The curved or bent section of the hook just behind the shank.

Hook eye   The closed loop at the end of the shank to which the leader or the tippet is attached.

Hook keeper   The small wire loop attached to the fly rod just above the handle. It is used to place the fly out of harm's way when the rod, reel, line, and leader are not in use but still assembled.

Hook shank   The length of the wire of a fly hook exclusive of the eye and bend. This is the section to which the imitation fly materials are tied.

Hook size   The distance or amount of gap on a fly hook or fly. Size also refers to the overall length and size of wire that the hook is made from. Hook sizes range from the smallest, No. 36, to the largest, No. 5/0.

Hopper   An imitation fly simulating a grasshopper.

Horse   The process of pulling or yanking the fly line after a fish has been hooked in an attempt to land the fish. In most cases, trying to horse a fish in results in losing the fish and/or leader and fly.

Ichthyologist   A specialist in that branch of zoology that deals with fish.

Imago   Insect in its final adult mature winged state.

Inlet   That part of a lake or ocean where a river or stream enters the larger body of water.

Jack   A nickname for mature one- or two-year-old rainbow trout, steelhead, or salmon that run with older fish in their spawning run.

Jump   When a hooked fish leaps up out of the water in an attempt to shake the hook or break the line.

Knotless   A leader that has no knots in it to join the different sizes of leader sections or tippets. Also called a tapered leader.

Kyping   The hooked nose developed by males (chinook salmon) ready to make spawning runs.

Landing   Netting, beaching, or capturing a fish after it has been hooked and given up the struggle to shake the hook.

Larva   The wormlike stage between the egg and pupa of the caddis and midge aquatic insects. It also refers to the artificial-fly imitation of the larva called nymph.

Lateral line   A connected series of receptors on the side of a fish that are sensitive to vibrations and low-frequency movements under the water. These sensitive receptors warn the fish of other predators in the water or the presence of foreign bodies in the water.

Leader   The transparent part of the fly-fishing line between the fly line and the fly. Most leaders are tapered, with the largest-diameter butt end attached to the fly line and the thinnest part (tippet) attached to the fly.

Leader shy   Fish that are suspicious and even spooked by the sight of the leader or tippet of a fly line.

Leader wallet   A convenient and compact container for storage of extra leaders to be carried while fly-fishing.

Line   The fly line used for fly-fishing. There are many types of fly line: floating, sinking, tapered, weight forward, etc. Each one is designed for the particular type of fishing.

Line guard   The part of a fly-rod reel that the fly line passes through or over as it is wound on or off the reel spool. It acts as a guide and reduces wear from line friction.

Loop   The U shape of the fly line as it unrolls with the forward cast or backward cast. Wide loops cause problems. Tight loops allow more control of the cast.

Loop to loop   The joining of fly line to leader or leader to tippet with one loop fastened to the other loop.

Low-water slack   The period between the flood tide (high coming in) and the ebb tide (going out) when the water is at the low point and not moving.

Lure   An imitation fish food with hooks attached with colors and shapes to attract fish to strike.

Mature insect   Insects that have reached sexual maturity or full growth.

Meadow river   A slow-moving, meandering stream usually located in a piedmont plane or valley.

Mending   Correcting the large curvature of the fly line on the water caused by the wind and the water current. If not corrected, the fly will be pulled unnaturally and spook the fish. Correction is made by flipping the curved line with the rod tip.

Milt   The sperm-containing fluid of a male fish.

Minnow   Any small fish 1/2–8 inches long, which includes the fry and fingerlings of game fish.

Monofilament   A single strand of nylon or other plastic material used for fishing line, leaders, or tippets.

Morphology   A branch of biology that deals with the form and structure of fish, insects, animals, and plants.

Moss bed   An underwater growth of aquatic plants.

Muddler   An artificial fly that is very popular. It has a large, clipped deer-hair head with hair and feathers for its body and wings.

Neap tides   Tides that occur during the first and third quarter phase of the moon that result in a minimum rise and fall of the tides. The position of the sun and the moon are at 90 degrees to the earth.

Neck   A long, narrow body of water found most of the time at a river's inlet to a lake or tidal basin.

Net   A large open-weave fabric mounted in a wooden or aluminum frame used to capture fish that have been hooked, tired out, and brought to the angler after the fish has struggled for its freedom.

Neutral color   The color and pattern of an artificial fly that does not contrast with its natural surroundings.

No kill   A fishing policy of catching and releasing fish unharmed back into the water.

Nymph   A water-breathing or immature stage of aquatic insects. Also an artificial fly that imitates these insects.

Nymphing   Fly-fishing with artificial fly imitations of nymphs.

Outlet   That part of a lake or pond that discharges into a waterway, usually a stream or river.

Panfish   A large group of freshwater game fish, most of which are under 2 pounds in weight. These include sunfish, bluegill, bream, yellow perch, crappie, rock bass, etc.

Parr   The second stage of development of salmonoids, usually called fingerlings.

Pectoral fin   Fins mounted just behind the gills of a fish. Used primarily for steering.

Pelagic fish   Those fish that can live and feed well above the bottom.

Perch   A group of fish, including the yellow perch, white perch, darters, and walleyed pike.

Pickup   Lifting of the fly line, leader, and fly off the water as the backcast is started.

Pike   A class of cool freshwater game fish that includes northern pike, pickerel, and muskie.

Piscatory   Relating to or dependent on fishing or fishermen.

Piscivorous   Fish that feed on other fish.

Plankton   Microscopic-size animals that float and drift in the water of lakes, seas, rivers, and streams. Many small larvae, minute plants, crustaceans, and some mollusk and worms make up a plankton population.

Poacher   One who takes fish (or game) illegally.

Pocket   A depression in the bottom of a stream located in the riffle or the run of a river or stream.

Point   The narrow, pointed section of land that juts out into a lake or stream.

Polarize   To cause light rays to vibrate in such a manner as to eliminate glare from the water surface and cause fish, logs, and other underwater structures to become more visible.

Pond   A small open body of water usually less than five acres in surface area.

Pound test   A measurement of the strength of a fishing line, leader, or tippet. Also called breaking strength.

Popper   A relatively large artificial fly used mostly for fishing for bluegill or bass that delivers a "pop" when retrieved with a short pull on the fly line. It is supposed to imitate a wounded mayfly, moth, or even a mouse.

Power   Used to describe the amount of energy expended with the wrist and arm movement when casting a fly line with the fly rod.

Predator fish   A fish that eats other fish, insects, or animals.

Presentation   The placement of the artificial fly on or under the water. Also, the path of the fly through the air and on the water.

Pumping fish   Pulling up a large fish with a rod-lifting action as the fish dives or moves away. When the rod is lowered after pumping up, the reel takes up the slack line gained from pumping the fish.

Punch list   A checklist of essential items needed or desired for a special operation, expedition, or journey.

Pupa   The stage between egg and adult of aquatic insects or an artificial fly (nymph) that imitates the pupa.

Put and take   A fish-management policy of stocking legal-size fish in a pond or stream and then removing these fish when they are caught.

Rapids   A section of a stream or river that has a steep gradient (slope) with fast, rough, and turbulent water.

Reading the water   A visual examination of the surface and depth of the water of a stream, lake, or pond to evaluate the fishing potential.

Reel   A mechanism with a revolving spindle turned by a crank handle used to store a fly line on a fly rod. The line is usually stripped from the reel by pulling it by hand; then it is cast with the fly rod.

Reel saddle   The part of a reel that provides a means of mounting the reel onto the rod seat of the fly rod.

Reel seat   That part of a fly rod just behind the rod handle where the reel is mounted and secured.

Reel spool   The spindle of a fly-rod reel where the backing and fly line are wound and stored.

Riffle water   The section of a river or stream where the water is relatively shallow and the flow is irregular, with the surface being rough and turbulent. Usually caused by submerged obstructions, such as gravel, rocks, logs, etc.

Rig   A complete assembly of items and/or equipment for a specific task, such as fishing gear, boat, trailer and motor, or horse and buggy.

Rising fish   Fish that are visibly feeding at or just below the surface of the water.

Rod   A long wand or stick made up of a handle, seat for a reel, and guides for a fly line assembled for the purpose of casting a fly line and artificial fly to catch a fish. Modern rods are made of fiberglass, bamboo, graphite, or some combination thereof.

Rod guides   The closed-loop structures fastened along the length of the fly rod that hold the fly line close to the rod all along its length. The first guide just above the handle is the stripper guide, which receives most of the wear from stripping the fly line during the retrieve from a cast. The other guides are called the snake guides.

Run   The running swim a fish makes when it is trying to escape after being hooked. Also the stretch of a stream just below a riffle and above the pool.

Salmon fly   An artificial fly used to catch salmon. Also a name given to many large aquatic stone fly insects.

Saltwater fly   An artificial fly made to be fished in salt water. The hook must resist saltwater corrosion.

Selective   Refers to the feeding habits of fish, which prefer special flies, or a special presentation of flies.

School   A group of the same species of fish swimming together.

Scud   A small shrimplike crustacean or an artificial fly imitating the crustacean.

Shoal   A shallow bottom area in a lake, stream, or tidal flat. Very often dangerous to boating.

Shooting   The act of casting out the fly line with sufficient force caused by the momentum created by the action of the fly rod with the weight of the fly line.

Shoreline   The land area adjoining the edge of the water of a lake or river.

Shrimp   An important crustacean and its artificial fly imitation.

Skater   A floating artificial fly with a very long hackle or hair around the hook so it can sit high and skate across the surface of the water.

Slack line   When the fly line has little or no tension on it between the reel, rod, and the fly.

Slack tide   The period between high tide (flood tide) and low tide (ebb tide) when the water is not moving.

Smolts   Young, six-inch-long first-year salmon.

Snake guide   An open-wire loop attached to a fly rod to hold the fly line close to the shaft of the fly rod.

Soft strike   The taking of an artificial fly by a fish by merely inhaling the fly into its mouth instead of biting it with its teeth and jaw. Many times such a strike is imperceptible except for a slight disturbance in the line. A strike indicator is therefore needed when fishing nymphs underwater so the hook can be set before the fish spits out the fly.

Snelled fly   A fly with a short piece of monofilament attached to it. On the other end of the monofilament line is a fixed loop to attach the snell to the leader.

Spawn   The process of fish reproduction. Also a mass of fish eggs.

Spawning   Fish reproduction process; usually occurs during the spring or fall in the lakes and rivers.

Species   A category of biological classification ranking just below the genus or subgenus and comprising related organisms or populations capable of interbreeding. Of interest to anglers for the different species of fish and/or insects.

Spillway   The downstream face of a dam where the water is discharged usually at a predetermined rate of flow. The control mechanism of the spillway regulates the outflows from the reservoir. Regulated to satisfy electric power and irrigation requirements, the variation of spillway discharge has an enormous impact on fish habitat and populations.

Spinner The adult stage (imago) of mayfly aquatic insects. Imagoes (spinners) will swarm over the waters in great numbers to mate and lay eggs. These swarms may number in the millions at the time of a given hatch.

Spinning A method of casting a lure with a rod and a fixed-spool casting reel in which the line spins off the fixed reel because the weighted lure is pulling the line from the reel.

Splice Joining two fly-line sections together.

Spook To frighten a fish so much that it stops feeding or swims away and hides.

Spring tides These are extremely high and low tides that occur twice a month during the full and new moons when the sun, moon, and the earth are aligned in a straight line. Normally this is the best time for saltwater fly-fishing in the surf and inshore flats.

Stand Dead water or slack between the flood tide and the ebb tide.

Standing end The main fishing line or leader to which terminal tackle is tied.

Steelhead A migrating rainbow trout that lives most of its life in large freshwater lakes or oceans and returns to the rivers or streams where it was born in order to reproduce or sometimes to feed. These fish are generally much larger than the rainbows that do not migrate from the streams.

Steelhead fly An artificial fly designed for catching steelhead.

Streamer An artificial wet fly that imitates a minnow or small fish.

Strategy The art of devising a carefully thought out plan for the purpose of achieving a specific goal, namely, a fishing expedition.

Strike A fish hitting or biting the artificial fly presented by the angler. Also, the action the angler takes to set the hook once the fish has taken the fly.

Stringer A length of rope, cord, or chain used to keep fish alive in the water after they have been caught.

Stripper guide   The first large guide on the butt section above the handle on a fly rod. It is designed to reduce friction on the fly line when it is cast out or stripped in a retrieve.

Stripping   The act of rapidly retrieving a fly and fly line by making a series of pulls on the line with the line hand. This procedure is also used for stripping the line from the reel in preparation for a forward cast.

Structure   Different objects in the water that provide cover and resting places for fish. A typical structure would be large rocks, dock pilings, logs, sunken boats, etc.

Subimago   Immature aquatic insect form that has shed its skin so it can fly.

Studs   Lugs or protrusions of hard rubber or metal on the bottom of wading boots to provide additional traction for walking or wading over gravel, slippery rocks, logs, or other underwater debris.

Swim   The locomotion of a wet fly as it moves through the water when it is being fished. It may move like a wounded minnow, a nymph, or a dead spinner.

Synthetic fly-tying material   The materials for tying artificial flies that are man-made, such as Orlon, nylon, etc.

Tackle   The general term for all of the fishing equipment used by the angler for fly-fishing, such as rod, reel, line, leaders, tippets, flies, creel, boots, etc.

Tactics   The art and skill of employing available knowledge, fishing tackle, and other resources for the accomplishment of a specific goal. Tactics are employed as part of an overall strategy.

Tag end   The short end of a line or leader remaining after a knot has been tied joining the longer line to a fly, leader, tippet, etc.

Tail   The caudal fin of a fish or the lower end of a pond, stream, or the discharge from the spillway of a dam; also called a tailrace.

Tailer   A tool for landing fish. It has a locking loop on the handle that locks around the tail of a fish.

Tailing A term used to describe a fish feeding in a position along the bottom in shallow water so that its tail is visible above the surface of the water.

Tailwater The stream coming from the downstream face or the spillway of a dam. Also called a tailrace.

Tailwater trout Trout that live in the tailwater of a dam.

Take The action of a fish catching some food or a fly.

Taper The reduction or increase of the diameter of a line or leader. Many fly rods are also tapered.

Terrestrial Insects whose life cycle takes place on dry land. The most common insects are grasshoppers, ants, crickets, and beetles that are often blown by the wind onto the water of a stream or lake.

Tide The periodic rising and lowering of water levels in rivers, lakes, and especially oceans or tidal flats due to the gravitational forces of the sun and the moon. These movements occur twice a day and vary in magnitude, depending on the location of the body of water on the earth. Fish feeding is enhanced at the ebb tide, or when the tide is coming in.

Tie The process of fastening lines, leaders, etc., together with the proper knots. It is also the term for assembly of fur, feathers, yarn, and hooks to make an artificial fly.

Tippet The small end of a leader or additional section of monofilament tied to the end of the leader.

Tip top The fly-rod line guide that is fitted over the tip end of the rod.

Treble hook Three fishhooks that are joined to one common shank.

Trolling Fishing an artificial fly or a lure behind a moving boat.

Trout Any of the various fishes of the family Salmonidae, but smaller than the typical salmon. Trout are restricted to cool, clear fresh water with a high oxygen content. The most common types are brook, brown, rainbow, and cutthroat trout.

Twitch   A small movement given to the artificial fly by using the rod tip or a short fly-line strip.

Vest (fishing)   A vestlike garment containing a number of various-size pockets used to carry essential flies and other desirable fishing accessories while fly-fishing.

Wading   Walking in a river, stream, lake, or tidal flat in water no deeper than your chest.

Waders   Waterproof boots that extend up above the waistline.

Wading staff   A stout stick used to assist the angler in wading in swift water and/or slippery bottoms of streams.

Warm-water fish   Fish that thrive best in water temperatures of 65–85 degrees Fahrenheit.

Water conditions   A description of the water, including the level of the water, the temperature of the water, the wind conditions, and the clarity of the water.

Weed guard   A nylon or metal wire attached to the shank of the hook of an artificial fly to prevent the hook from catching weeds and vegetation in the fishing area.

Wiggle nymph   A hinged two-section artificial nymph fly that wiggles when pulled through the water.

Wind knot   A troublesome overhand knot that is accidentally tied on the fly line when casting.

Wooly worm   A sinking artificial fly that has a fuzzy or wooly body and hackle spiraled around and over the length of the fly. This is also the larva (caterpilar) of terrestrial moths or butterflies.